What About Learning?

Edited by David Grant, Saba Salekfard, and Nina Rappaport

Eero Saarinen Visiting Professorship, Yale School of Architecture

Deborah Saunt with Jane Wong and Timothy Newton

Yale School of Architecture
180 York Street
New Haven, CT 06520
www.architecture.yale.edu

Distributed by Actar
440 Park Ave. South, 17th fl.
New York, NY 10016
www.actar.com

Director of Publications: Nina Rappaport
Editors: David Grant, Saba Salekfard, and Nina Rappaport
Text Editor: Ann Holcomb
Design to the concept by Sarah Gephart MGMT Design
ISBN: 978-1-63840-082-0

The Eero Saarinen Visiting Professorship was
established in 1984 through the generosity and
efforts of the architect Kevin Roche in honor of Eero
Saarinen, who received a BArch from Yale in 1934.
This endowed chair enables the School to invite
a distinguished architect to teach a design studio
each term.

Contents

"What about Learning?"

Introduction

Deborah Saunt
Eero Saarinen Visiting Professor

Operating between academic discourse and the realities of practice, lived experiences, and co-produced knowledge, the "What About Learning?" advanced architecture studio at Yale asked how we can better share knowledge of our built and natural environment. As much as the studio was interested in the historic urban fabric and the physical context of a site, it also championed strategic research and thinking that also considered the nonphysical networks and less tangible conditions and behaviors that may unlock latent spatial potential to produce more radical and responsive architectures. In the process, students consciously challenged the conventions of architectural practice, pushed the envelope of the role of the architect or urban designer, and took on alternative roles such as "spatial strategists" and "designer-activists." Valuing the inherent wealth of collective knowledge and the everyday that students brought with them to the table, the studio provided a platform for students to shape their own personal research agency and design briefs based on their individual preoccupations and understanding of themselves as both designers and citizens in the world. The influence of the studio has informed further research into the very nature of what constitutes the relevance of existing architectural education and what constitutes a school of architecture.

Underpinning the principles and methodologies of the studio was the idea of spatial justice shaping a conceptual framework that addresses the intersectionality of multiple concerns—racial injustice, environmental crisis, health in equity, etc.—and informs more equitable spatial practices. Spatial justice, at its core, provides an opportunity for people, architects, and designers to carve out spaces that give agency and power to the seldom heard and disenfranchised and facilitates a sense of belonging for those treated as outsiders. It is about increasing accessibility and facilitating adequate representation—not just in the built environment but in the city-making process—and creating platforms for people to have authorship over their shared spaces and how they are shaped over time. Spatial justice presents an opportunity for architecture to truly serve and be informed by the needs of the diverse inhabitants of our cities.

Against the backdrop of the COVID-19 pandemic, the studio focused on the relationships between dispersed learning and the right to the city, uncovering and reflecting on the human cost, challenges, and opportunities made evident over the course of "remote learning" across institutions worldwide. While the global experiment of remote learning appeared to have unlocked possibilities of overcoming mobility injustices by digitally connecting more students with educational resources, it has in many ways fallen short of redistributing power between institutions and their co-located communities. "What About Learning?" is fundamentally a question about the right to access knowledge and how our cities, buildings, and public spaces are controlled and shaped, and with it, the right to participate in civic life. With the neoliberal turn in education, learning as a lifelong activity has become codified and commercialized by educational institutions that operate within existing market conditions and infrastructures of knowledge distribution. By seamlessly blending into the digital fabric of consumerist life, much of learning has lost its intrinsic relationship to the communal spatial experience of knowledge production and its ability to challenge its own complicity. Between disembodied learning and a renewed sense of civic participation on the streets, the architectural question is, what is the site for learning today, and what are the alternative forms of learning and exchange it could nurture?

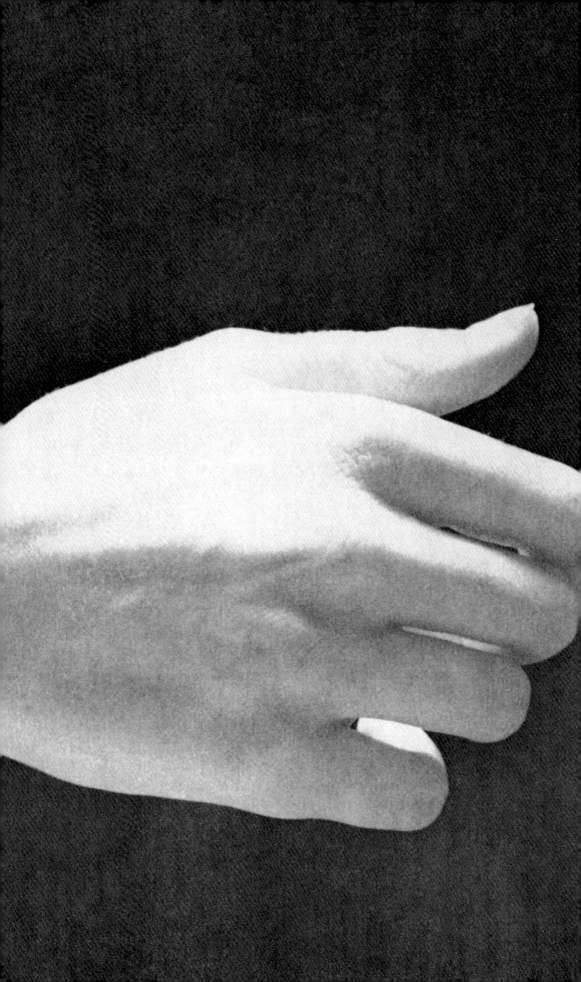

At a time no less tumultuous, Cedric Price's May 1968 *AD* issue, titled "What about Learning?," offered a poignant critique of education structures and institutional learning at large. His prescient editorial warned against the lack of criticality in the architecture profession with regards to the designing of spaces for education and pedagogical principles that—though they perpetuate political, social, and economic injustices—are still rarely questioned. Today's ongoing crises and protest movements have created a new impetus to question the ethical and spatial relationships of educational institutions around diversity, the climate, and the recent pandemic. When the Yale campus was under lockdown, it extended out virtually from Rudolph Hall to the geographically dispersed private spaces of students and professors, raising radical questions of communication, mobility, and participation in knowledge production and design. As an architecture studio, having mapped out traditional academic settings and our lockdown ones, we looked beyond bricks and mortar and also applied our spatial intelligence to the analysis of wider environmental, political, and socioeconomic relationships in learning and how they manifest across urban contexts and virtual environments.

With the blurring of private and communal boundaries, the new forms of learning present difficult spatial and ethical relationships and are open to new risks and contingencies. The spatial strategies of the 1960s and '70s, which promised open access and further democratization, have been increasingly appropriated in privatized institutions and, more recently, been adopted ubiquitously in remote working. Such forms of appropriation, where education becomes pure dissemination confined within a closed loop of networks rather than a speculative environment for consolidation and innovation, undermine knowledge exchange in learning. Emerging from current crises that plainly underscore deep-rooted inequalities and injustices, our task today is to envision new forms of participation and engagement in spatial practices that will reestablish reciprocity between knowledge and civic life. Regenerative spaces for learning will enable exchange, participation, and the exercise of political rights where public life will be sustained, nurtured, and enriched by discourse and educational empowerment.

Left: "What about Learning?" *Architectural Design,* May 1968 issue,
guest-edited by Cedric Price

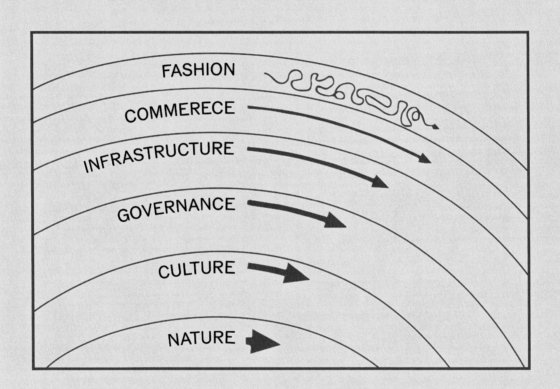

FASHION

COMMERECE

INFRASTRUCTURE

GOVERNANCE

CULTURE

NATURE

Top: Pace layering diagram adapted from Stewart Brand, DSDHA

Studio Description

Deborah Saunt with Jane Wong

Introduction

In 2020–2022, COVID-19, Black Lives Matter, and the climate emergency brought into focus urgent questions about education and the built environment and their roles in shaping democratic life. What, how, and where we learn are political issues mediated through spatial conditions—"sites of learning"—that shape processes in knowledge dissemination, production, and exchange.

The site of learning does not refer merely to its physical space, but to its wider networked relationships to resources and users and the power of those connections to determine one's place in the world. Taking learning outside privileged enclaves and looking at more contemporary, dispersed learning, we considered parallel territories and alternative sites where new encounters can take place and where collective experiences of knowledge production and locally embedded exchange can be cultivated.

At the beginning of the semester, students identified their own sites of personal relevance based on appraisal of their hybrid physical-virtual architectural learning experiences. Reflecting upon the multitude of "publics" in their "geographies of now," students then selected an area or series of spaces that could be considered as shared territories for emergent models of learning. By applying spatial intelligence and a "pace-layered" approach to uncover wider shared learning potentials,[1] they analyzed associated infrastructures and latent networks at different scales with respect to jurisdiction, accessibility, and impact. The emerging sites of learning—shared spaces where people might like plazas, parks, parking lots, et al.—were then reinterpreted to enable new pedagogical models based on inherent function and spatial potential, providing maximum social benefit and value: "The best for the most for the least," as the Eamesian principle asserts.

The students then surveyed and reassessed radical pedagogical models and sites of architectural learning across history, starting with the Yale School of Architecture and considering architecture in the widest sense to encompass interdisciplinary practices. We followed the trajectories of alternative learning models, tracing them back to their conceptual genealogies, one of which was the London School of Architecture (LSA) for which Deborah Saunt is a founding director. Our line of inquiry resonated with the university model of eleventh- to twelfth-century Paris, where the whole city was the campus, and the urban art-collective approach of the Independent Group of the 1950s (Eduardo Paolozzi, Peter and Alison Smithson, Peter Reyner Banham, et al.). Pedagogical and spatial tools were assessed and reinterpreted with consideration to their sites and wider networks. With the dispersed learning of Cedric Price's 1966 Potteries Thinkbelt project and the city-as-curriculum from Denise Scott Brown, Robert Venturi, and Steven Izenour's 1967 Learning from Las Vegas studio as key precedents, we proposed new forms of learning where the site is intrinsic to knowledge production, and knowledge production generates new democratic spaces that accelerate public agency in influencing and shaping them.

[1] Stewart Brand, "Pace Layering: How Complex Systems Learn and Keep Learning," *Journal of Design and Science*, Jan. 27, 2018. https://doi.org/10.21428/7f2e5f08

Studio Organization

The studio was organized in three stages:

1–Research thesis development, site selection, and analysis

2–Proposition, pedagogical tools, and spatial strategy

3–Detailed architectural design and representation

The first began with a series of seminars and workshops where we studied, as a collective, precedents of alternative learning models and physical sites of architectural learning, including the Yale School of Architecture itself. In parallel, students selected individual sites for their projects, where they assessed how a new form of learning would generate a potential future template for learning, and defined their thesis based on their site analysis and personal learning experiences combined with the studio's collective research.

At the second stage, students developed individual propositions for alternative learning through the translation of pedagogical tools to spatial devices. Spatial strategies were then developed for different scales of the project, from strategic to local to building.

At the third stage, students developed their specific architectural design and representation. The resolution of the design proposals differed depending on the nature of each individual project, and students were encouraged to develop forms of representation that reflected specific subject matters and proposals.

Alternative Learning Models

The Prophecy of the Learning Network: The Potteries Thinkbelt

In May 1968, at the cusp of the student movements that would usher in a decade of radical political and cultural discourse, *AD* published "What about Learning?", a seminal issue guest-edited by Cedric Price on the problems of contemporary education. The journal's cover featured Price's collage of a televised image over the clock face of a wristwatch, one of his many prophetic provocations that anticipated the total acclimatization of everyday life to digital technology and virtual networks. Price believed in the emancipatory potential of learning and sought to liberate the lifelong activity from its temporal, spatial, and institutional structures, a major theme that runs through his work—from Polyark, the mobile school of architecture, to Atom, a system of dispersed educational units across the town.[2]

Potteries Thinkbelt (1963–1967), or "PTb," put forward a radical critique of the existing model of higher education as an isolated enterprise hosted in polite cathedral-town amenities, with a curriculum and organization divorced from their wider communities, much as it is today. PTb was conceived as a learning network that appropriated existing public infrastructure—regional road and railway links—to facilitate flexible learning for 20,000 students and faculty members who traveled across the network to learn in different educational establishments and lodged in temporary housing embedded within local communities. Where physical exchange was not important, individual study was enabled by electronic communication systems. The traditional functions of the university were reinterpreted and redistributed across the network, with new typologies for faculty areas and housing and "transfer areas" of large laboratories and workshops. Yet for all its technological novelties, PTb was premised upon a basic economic principle often neglected in appraisals of this project, which is that under this proposed network of learning students are to be paid for their work. Price argued that student loans and the wider financial model of higher education drew a separation between the students and the wider community, and proposed publicly funded salaries as an alternative.[3]

Today, proliferating learning networks, some bearing uncanny similarities to those suggested in PTb, exploit the flexibility and expediency of dispersed modes of learning, yet the status of the student is relegated to that of a consumer,[4] with an accompanying erosion of education's infrastructural role for public good. The Bologna Declaration[5] of 1999, while promising unprecedented mobility for students across the EU, introduced wholesale standardization processes that oriented learning towards qualification and aligned the knowledge industry with market forces, creating the "most competitive knowledge economy in the world." Today the communitarian values espoused by PTb are undone in hyperconnected academic circuits and virtual learning where students move within closed networks accessible only to those who can pay, networks that depend on support structures and tools—accommodation, electricity, the computer, the internet—wholly funded by students themselves.

At this impasse, PTb could be criticized for its unquestioned faith in the emancipatory potential of dispersed learning, however its relevance today lies in its first critical question, what is the site for learning today? Building upon this question in the context of contested education networks, we asked the students what alternative networks and wider global challenges can be identified and reimagined to open new forms of access and exchange.

[2] From Cedric Price's editorial essay in "What about Learning?" *Architectural Design*, May 1968

[3] From Cedric Price's "National School Plan," 1966

[4] For American context: A. J. Angulo, *Diploma Mills: How For-Profit Colleges Stiffed Students, Taxpayers, and the American Dream* (Baltimore: Johns Hopkins University Press, 2016).

[5] Joint declaration of the European Ministers of Education from 29 European states, adopted in 1999 as part of the Bologna Process, a series of meetings and agreements to ensure comparability in the standards and quality of higher-education qualifications.

Top: The Journey to Tahiti, Kassel, 1987   Bottom: Motorists' Walk, Seminar Perception and Traffic, Kassel 1993

Top left: Students using the Open University S100 home experiment kit, c.1970

Top right: The McArthur microscope

Bottom: M201 Filming

Next page: Car View of the Strip with Robert Venturi and Denise Scott Brown, 1968

Site as Curriculum: Learning from the Road

The road trip would eventually transform architectural history, education, and design values, and was introduced in the fall of 1968 as part of the Learning Las Vegas studio at Yale, just a few months after the publication of Cedric Price's "What about Learning?". The transatlantic confluences were not accidental. In fact, Cedric Price and Robert Venturi certainly met the year before, at the Rice Design Fête in Houston, Texas, a twelve-day-long charrette on the subject of New Schools for New Towns, organized at the School of Architecture at Rice University. Price and Venturi's teams developed divergent schemes, with the total dispersal of learning facilities in Price's decentralized model, and the centralized "educational strip" in Venturi's, prefacing the radical affirmation of The Strip as the site and subject of architectural learning in the Learning from Las Vegas studio.

The following year, Denise Scott Brown proposed a new studio at Yale, with the intent of interrogating The Strip as "a very large as-found object," embracing the totality of its commercial vernacular and iconographic phenomena. Together with Venturi and Steven Izenour, an MED student at Yale, Scott Brown led students to exhaust all forms of media in documenting the city, from film and photography to diagrams and maps, some of which were generated from imagery captured via a borrowed helicopter. The studio's approach was challenged by fellow faculty members who regarded its indiscriminate embrace of the total environment of popular consumerism dubious. Indeed, the success of the studio's iconography overshadowed its critical lessons on engaging here-and-now with the ordinary and the everyday as an integral part of a design process that is so valued today. Learning from Las Vegas as an alternative learning model positioned the site as the central subject of study—the site was the curriculum—and left open-ended the question of design being solely a physical outcome.

Scott Brown articulated this pedagogical attitude in the working sessions of the Universitas Project (1972), a symposium dedicated to the formation of a new university of design concerned with the man-made milieu. In the company of speakers and participants ranging from Hannah Arendt to Henri Lefebvre, Scott Brown remarked:

I think we should be discussing the design of instruments that would elicit new values, or asking ourselves what types of instruments could help mediate value conflicts.[6]

The Learning studios took place against the backdrop of the Civil Rights Movement, worldwide student protests, and the destructive fire in the Yale Art & Architecture building in 1969. At no less critical a juncture of racial and climate injustices and the pandemic, we asked ourselves, what alternative learning instruments might we employ and what new values could be elicited in the reframing of our present realities? How do we remake our site of learning today?

[6] *The Universitas Project: Solutions for a Post-technological Society,*
Museum of Modern Art (MOMA), January 1972

Top: "Learning from Kilburn" was a roving "tiny experimental university" which used Kilburn High Road and its surrounds, such as the Tin Tabernacle, as a campus, occupying a number of locations for classes led by architects, artists, writers and thinkers during the fall and spring terms of 2013–14. The project was developed and directed by Tom Ó Caollaí, commissioned by Spacemakers, in collaboration with OK-RM and Pernilla Ohrstedt Studio. The project was funded by the London Boroughs of Brent and Camden.

Bottom four: An instantly deployable classroom set, providing a functional and unifying backdrop to the classes at any given site. Drawing on Kilburn curriculum and campus, the university offers a series of free classes, each led by a range of artists, architects, and thinkers.

Studio Symposium

In September 2020, due to prohibitive COVID-19-related travel restrictions, instead of the traditional field trip, the studio hosted a three-day symposium with a panel of international speakers who presented wide-ranging alternative models of learning and knowledge sharing as a spatial practice in the expanded field. The sessions were structured around the themes of pedagogy, activism, and art and community within the built environment. Virtual meeting platforms allowed a diverse audience consisting not only of students but members of the public to engage across vastly different time zones, with brilliant contributions from educators, practitioners, and provocateurs working in varied contexts. Speakers included Nelly Ben Hayoun-Stépanian, Mel Dodd, Beatrice Galilee, Sam Jacob, Lesley Lokko, Leroy Street Studio, Roberta Marcaccio, Joel de Mowbray, Alicia Pivaro, RESOLVE Collective, and Neal Shasore. Throughout the symposium, students' individual theses on alternative models of learning were discussed in working sessions.

Alicia Pivaro
London School of Architecture

Alicia is an urbanist, community activist, and artist working across disciplines and using participation and radical thinking to inform methods of urban and social change. After training as an architect, she worked at several leading organizations, including the London Arts Council (LAC), the Royal Institute of British Architects (RIBA), and the Architecture Foundation, where she developed projects that supported alternative practices, diverse voices, and community involvement in architectural discourse. She is an advocate for neighborhood planning and other examples of co-production of the city that work towards creating a more sustainable, equitable, and lovely version of the world.

Nelly Ben Hayoun-Stépanian, PhD
Nelly Ben Hayoun Studios

Award-winning designer of experiences Nelly Ben Hayoun-Stépanian has been manufacturing the impossible for over a decade. Advocating for plurality, she creates multi-dimensional transdisciplinary projects at the intersection of events, film, science, tech, theater, politics, music, and design with community engagement and accessibility at their core. To this end, she is a senior fellow of the Hannah Arendt Center. In 2017, Nelly founded The University of the Underground, a tuition-free university that supports free, pluralistic, and transnational education from the basement of nightclubs. She is the vice chair of the International Astronautical Federation (IAF) and the IAF's Committee for the Cultural Utilization of Space (ITACCUS). Nelly is the author and director of five feature-length documentaries investigating topics such as the origins of knowledge and totalitarian regimes. Her films work to platform diasporic and queer ecofeminist visions, which include *Tour de moon* (2023) and *Doppelgängers[3]* (2024). *Wired* awarded Nelly their inaugural Innovation Fellowship, *Icon* magazine named her as one of the top 50 designers shaping the future, and in June 2023 *Design Week* awarded her with their Lifetime Achievement Award.

Mel Dodd
Monash University

Mel Dodd is an architect and academic. Educated at the University of Cambridge and with a PhD By Practice (2011) from the Royal Melbourne Institute of Technology (RMIT), she has led architecture at a range of institutions since 1995 including The School of Art, Architecture, and Design at London Metropolitan University, RMIT University in Melbourne, and most recently Spatial Practices at Central Saint Martins, University of the Arts London, where in her role as associate dean she explores innovative partnerships between the university, external agencies, and communities. Her pedagogical practice focuses on the relationship between academia and practice, specifically within contested urban regeneration contexts. This subject is explored in her books, *Live Projects: Designing with People* (RMIT Press, 2012) and *Spatial Practices: Modes of Action and Engagement with the City* (Routledge, 2019).

Joel De Mowbray
Yes Make

Joel De Mowbray is an urban designer-maker combining experience as a local government officer in London with practical carpentry, construction, and sculpting skills. He creates imaginative places from disused spaces. His combination of experience allows him to translate placemaking and environmental policy objectives into physical projects that local people can get sucked into and make for themselves.

Morgan Hare and Marc Turkel
Leroy Street Studio

Leroy Street Studio (LSS), based in New York, occupies two worlds: one focused on delivering basic human needs through participatory public design work in underserved communities, the other on making highly crafted, refined private buildings. They constantly grapple with the question of their role and responsibilities as architects.

Akil Scafe-Smith and Seth Amani Scafe-Smith
RESOLVE Collective

RESOLVE is an interdisciplinary design collective that combines architecture, engineering, technology, and art to address multiscalar social challenges. The collective was founded in 2016 by University College London (UCL) graduates Akil Scafe-Smith and Gameli Ladzekpo leading a project called Rebel Space for the Brixton Design Trail. Throughout 2017, the project delivered workshops, presentations, and projects, most notably conducting a design workshop with a school in Dagenham called If These Walls Could Talk. Collaboration and co-production were critical parts of its ethos and are seen as the first step towards realizing more equitable visions of change.

Roberta Marcaccio
Architectural Association School of Architecture

Roberta Marcaccio is an editor, educator, and researcher collaborating with various architectural practices. After studying at the Politecnico di Milano and the Architectural Association (AA), she held various editorial roles and teaching positions while working for a number of design studios and completing a Research Fellowship in the Built Environment awarded by the Royal Commission for the Exhibition of 1851. Her writings on historical and emerging modes of practice have been featured in the journals *AA Files* and *Blueprint*, and in the books *Real Estates* (Bedford Press, 2014) and *Erasmus Effect* (Quodlibet, 2014). She co-edited an issue of *Architectural Design*, "The Business of Research: Knowledge and Learning Redefined in Architectural Practice" (Wiley, May/June 2019), as well as the book *Architects After Architecture* (Routledge, 2020). She recently edited an English-language collection of writings by Ernesto Nathan Rogers (MIT Press, 2024).

NELLY BEN HAYOUN-STÉPANIAN

Student symposium participants had the following questions for symposium panelist Nelly Ben Hayoun-Stépanian (NBHS).

GORDAN JIANG

From Did I Generate Dark Energy in the Kitchen Sink? to the Soyuz Chair to nonlinear research seminars and the University of the Underground, your project scales continuously enlarge and more units become involved. How does this unit change affect the way you design a learning model?

NBHS

I wish it was proportional like this! I love your question, Gordon, because in a way it's a very mathematical question. It shows how we're formatted to think within rational models, as opposed to empirical ones. If you're going to make the assumption that there is a proportional correlation between a learning model and a scale of action, you fall within linear research as opposed to nonlinear, which I believe allows for serendipity and other forms of connections to nature and other learning methods. I'd like to rethink all existing systems as multiverses, this idea that you have a bubble that expands as you blow, and eventually a new model is going to exist. That's the way I like to think about a learning model, just like a lava light.

For me, the success of a learning model is when it can arrive at a wild place and get out of control—that, to me, is the excitement, when it allows space and facilitates radical imagination. I am passionate about working to build these multiverses within economics, politics, and society too. In the creative realm, these different realms do connect because everything is connected. In order to make a pluralistic platform that has multiple viewpoints, like the University of the Underground (which is a free, pluralistic, and transnational charity), you really need to start looking at models that are a bit more organic-looking, and learn from animals and bacteria, in fact. How bacteria learn is a fascinating question in and of itself.

TYLER KREBS

I am very interested in creating spaces that allow users to transcend. Most of your projects seem to be centered around giving the public something bizarre/inaccessible/dangerous in order to create a sublime experience. Are there any buildings you have seen or been in that have provided a similar feeling for you?

NBHS

This is true. Buildings can be terrifying, yet can also give you sublime experiences at times. I think there is a reason why architects have been so focused on building churches and defining some genre—whether it's Gothic or Roman—spending so much time trying to build things that elongate, that go towards the sky. This idea, that to address the sublime you need to go vertical, is fascinating to me. For someone who is fascinated by space and science and has been working a lot in that industry, I think that there is always a feat—mainly engineering, but also logistical—in trying to build things that are really elongated. La Sagrada Familia is mind-blowing when it comes to the idea of the sublime—the shapes, the forms. Everything about it is not only creative, but, on an emotional or spiritual level, absolutely stunning.

I was lucky enough to visit the Lascaux Caves as part of my latest movie, *I Am (Not) a Monster*. For me, the Lascaux Caves demonstrate that the human action of thinking exists because of creativity. We are able to think because we are able to create. Creation is at the origin of our capacity to formulate a thought. That is what I believe and partly the reason why I made *I Am (Not) a Monster*, to ask oracles around the world how thinking works. I believe this goes hand in hand with what is displayed in the unique and sublime Lascaux Caves. To try to reproduce a cave or other elevated space is of great interest to me.

Other spaces I have been lucky enough to go to include Chernobyl, the Aral Sea, Baikonur Cosmodrome, and other strange, deep underwater places. I think it's possible to imagine radical new spaces for habitation that are in permanent

Left: Nelly Ben Hayoun-Stépanian in *Shiny Gold*, their solo show at Gaîté Lyrique in Paris, an immersive experience designed to inspire curiosity through nonlinear learning.

transition. I am trying to define spaces that can move, morph, expand, and allow for a conversation with other species or the universe through static or white noise. Another place I would recommend that you experience is an anechoic chamber.

BEN THOMPSON
Does it matter who funds the University of the Underground? Would you accept funding from the Monsantos of the world, corporations that reinforce undesirable power structures?

NBHS
I think that's a very contemporary question. With the University of the Underground, our charity that provides free, pluralistic, and transnational education, we receive donations from citizens of the world but also corporations, such as the tech company WeTransfer, which was one of the founding members of the university, and they get tax deductions, as is standard.

Your question is also a controversial question as, technically, the good answer is to say, "Absolutely not, I would never get financing for any charities or any of my activities coming from sources

associated with exploitation or abuse." But there is an argument, one that maybe we don't want to hear when we are trying to be politically correct, Where in this world is money clean?

Right now, my team and I are directing and producing a nationwide festival that is supported by a nonprofit receiving its funds from the UK government treasury; therefore, it is directly funded by UK taxpayers. There is a lot of controversy around this festival in general, but there is also a controversy about the use of taxpayer money. For one, it has been controversial to accept this funding under leadership from the conservative party—regardless of it actually coming directly from the citizens—and, secondly, it is part of a debate around the use of public funds and what should or should not be considered public service.

Citizens should support radical imagination through the arts, nightlife creations, and culture, in addition to health and other sectors. There is, however, a lot to unpack in this issue because it's about capitalism and the system that finances and supports activities, charities, communities, and social movements. It's also about radical forms of

Top: The experiential work "Super K Sonic BOOOum" imagines what it would be like to experience a sonic boom—when a particle is traveling faster than the speed of light. On entering the installation, visitors put on helmets, white rubber shoes, and boiler suits. They board boats that transport them through a space filled with water and covered with silver balloons. Nelly Ben Hayoun-Stépanian, 2022

imagination fueled and supported by finance and currency directly connected to nation-states and governments.

The question really should be, What are the next alternative economic models that we need to start supporting and empowering? But, no, we're not going to receive money from sources that are obviously "dirty." The real question is, Are there any sources of funding that are, when you really trace it, completely clean and eco-sourced? Until we take up the charge of rethinking our economic model, we're just talking for talking's sake. There is a challenge at stake here, and that is coming up with the next economic model.

SABA SALEKFARD

What are the power structures that the University of the Underground had to modify in order to have an unconventional educational model?

NBHS

First, we had to establish ourselves as a community, as an institution, as an ensemble. This platform started as an idea, expanded into an ensemble, then was about "partners in crime," putting it together

like Sun Ra and his Arkestra. Then it was about actually thinking about the whole experience, in terms of what is different at this university from anywhere else. In the conventional model of a research practice, we looked at how there is a certain expectation from the elite and the educated. So it was very important to start thinking about what could be an alternative model that would appeal to a demographic that does not feel recognized or supported within the mainstream model. For me, it has been about the multicultural and the extremely innovative, such as the nightlife of an institution, and finding a way to empower that landscape to modify existing power structures and agendas.

I wanted to find a way to actually support nightlife creators and countercultures through education platforms. We still had to partner with an institution that offers a degree, because the degree was really important as well; that was a big piece of work. We had to collaborate with a hosted partner, which at the time was the Sandberg Institute in Amsterdam. From there, we outsourced the degree and made sure that students could have access both to the main university where they would get their degree and to the other space, the basement of a nightclub,

Top: For "Super K Sonic BOOOum", Nelly Ben Hayoun-Stépanian created a super-sized version of a Japanese neutrino observatory, a space where electrons and neutrinos—a type of fundamental particle that makes up the universe—collide to create giant explosions. Nelly Ben Hayoun-Stépanian, 2022

where they could collaborate and develop their projects.

In order to build this unconventional educational model, first you have to find the ensemble and put it together, but then there's this moment when you have to go beyond what you've learned to organize. When I founded the University of the Underground, I resigned from my job at Central Saint Martins, which was a very steady job towards professorship, then retirement. I cut myself off from that comfortable idea about what education basically was: students pay money and you provide them with feedback in a service relationship.

I knew I was venturing into unknown territory building this thing from scratch. One key element was, of course, the experience of the students themselves going through that education model. The first cohort at the University of the Underground found it extremely challenging for many reasons. The challenge to the power of the university posed by this free alternative education model was extremely violent. The relationship wasn't supportive in any way, and that meant that the student experience was chaotic and quite unbearable. I wasn't really clear as to what was happening at the time when we were just developing the model, but that, in itself, was a really good experience because we learned, and you learn by doing.

Right: "Moon Experiences" repurposed disused buildings within cities to create surreal and theatrical spaces. The experience was built over three stages of a non-linear narrative format. Each area's narrative was based on a different theme: Celebrations, Communication, and Arrival. "Moon Experiences" is part of Tour de Moon, a nationwide festival celebrating nightlife, new beginnings, and youth culture. Nelly Ben Hayoun-Stépanian, 2023

There is a gap that undermines how we teach architecture, a gap between the official version of an architect's tasks versus what architects really do. The Royal Institute of British Architects' (RIBA) description of an architect's work stages communicates the essential part of an architect's services as professional: project delivery, cost plans, quality management, construction, and the regulatory environment. But, problematically, technical knowledge is foregrounded at the expense of broader skills and capability, those of the policy maker, the entrepreneur, and even the activist.

Architectural education has tried to respond to this gap by providing other domains of knowledge left out of these professional descriptions— from history to theory, representation to critical thinking—while veering towards the experimental and speculative at the expense of the practical and site-specific. This has not only failed to bridge the gap, but sometimes created a self-referential and hermetic discourse within architectural education that only accentuates the division. What type of learning might bridge the academy and the world outside, and how in the process might we deliver the diverse technical, ethical, and practice-based knowledge inherent to the architectural profession more effectively?

Learning to engage in practice relies on gaining knowledge through "experiences" that rehearse practice in situ. Engaging in urban sites is, of course, a familiar part of architectural education via the design studio. However, experiential or "situated" learning goes a step further because it does not just simulate real scenarios. Rather than using a structure or model of the world to learn, acquiring skills here happens through participating in the world itself. Situated forms of learning

have much to offer architectural education, and in architecture programs there has been a burgeoning interest in "live" projects—forms of project-based learning that have a real client and a real site, and liaise with communities and agencies outside the university, engaging with practical, professional, ethical, and technical issues in a way that conventional education often fails to do. These learning experiences enshrine an outward-facing agenda that bridges the schism between the academy and practice.

At an institutional level, the ways in which a university can contribute to its local neighborhood is also increasingly important. Knowledge exchange that can translate research within universities into impact on society and the economy is particularly relevant for architecture and urban disciplines, and includes activities, processes, and skills that enable close collaboration between universities and external partner organizations to deliver environmental, cultural, and place-based benefits for both communities and students. A "civic" university—community-embedded and engaged in local innovation and knowledge generation— can contribute to a broader ecosystem in which overlapping domains of civil society, government, and industry are actively delivering place-based innovation.

Learning architectural and urban practice requires innovations in education that go beyond merely bridging the gap between academic frameworks of learning and the world outside. It requires a transformation of the way in which universities and their programs operate, embedding learning and research within external organizations and reconceptualizing students as producers and the academy as a civic university.

Top left : Contested Space Round Table Series at Central Saint Martins - UAL, a platform for open-ended talks, and critical debates intended to promote an exchange of ideas and questions exploring conceptual and disciplinary boundaries, and asking social and political questions.

Bottom left: Fire to Flourish Program—a service learning initiative at Monash University. Students supporting fire affected communities in resilience building through co-design for placemaking in Clarence Valley, NSW

Top: The Brooklyn Public Library Sunset Park is located in a former courthouse building and shares space with the NYPD and the local community board. The Sunset Park branch requires an interim library space to serve the community during the construction of a new library and affordable housing on its existing site. LSS, 2018

Bottom: In an LSS-led workshop, students created mobiles representing a range of themes they thought should be represented in their community's library—diversity, the future, and the neighborhood. LSS, 2018

Over the past 25 years, our firm Leroy Street Studio (LSS) has focused on drawing people directly into the process of making buildings. The joy of collaborating among clients, community, builders, and architects in a project's design and construction inspires us. We founded the nonprofit workshop Hester Street (HST) twenty years ago to foster a sustained commitment to this work in New York's Lower East Side. HST works with local stakeholders to understand their needs and implement physical changes in their public spaces.

Early projects building gardens with local elementary schools led to educational programs to transform public spaces in many schools. Working with community organizations on a plan to redevelop the East River waterfront led to a multiyear pop-up park, clinching public investment in open space. Navigating the city's bureaucracy around tight budgets for projects that often span many years demanded tenacity and commitment. Deeper participation with the community proved critical to understanding needs and the viability of physical changes to neighborhoods and buildings in the long term.

As HST evolved to focus on larger-scale social justice issues in community development and public policy, LSS continued to develop architectural processes to involve stakeholders and provide them with direct access. Projects such as the Sunset Park Library in Brooklyn and the East Village Homes gave residents opportunities to become more deeply involved in making new buildings. At the Sunset Park Library, LSS participated in a robust engagement process led by HST and community leaders, working with librarians, local nonprofit organizations, and students to design and fabricate large sunshade sculptures that transformed the space. At the East Village Homes affordable housing project, LSS worked with neighborhood high school students and the Grand Street Settlement to enhance the facade design. Through a series of workshops, students worked with architects to create original cladding elements derived from their memories and observations. The workshop's process—iterative, experimental, and educational—yielded functional elements that provide a highly visible connection to the Lower East Side streetscape while giving agency to community members.

These interventions represent a portion of the project budget and have an outsized impact. Our participatory design work reflects the power of intensively engaging stakeholders for collaborative projects that are central to our practice.

Taking a historical perspective on the long-standing relationship between the university and the city, I am raising questions about the contexts within which we locate the practice of learning.

At its beginning in the Middle Ages, the university was placeless. It was a network of individuals operating from different churches or theaters made available to them within a given city. Its scope was to help scholars "build their thesis" through a series of well-established techniques that would "stabilize" the wandering mind and help it "construct" an argument. The university thus had an architecture intended as a series of practices, but it didn't have a building. It also had no particular attachment to the city. The faculty and students—often regarded as "foreigners"—thought of the university as being portable, and considered it necessary to move from city to city to follow the great teachers. This remained true until 1322, when, for the first time, to prevent this highly mobile group of individuals from migrating elsewhere, the city of Paris provided a dedicated building for the students and faculty.

The building thus worked as a constraining device, forging ties between the university and the city and keeping the scholars' wandering body in place. From this point onwards, European universities were established as part of the urban scene and enjoyed the support of their host cities, which assumed the payment of salaries, provided loans, and regulated the book trade, lodgings, and all other services required by the students. Why? Because they brought money and renown to the city.

Top: With the Global Free Unit, Robert Mull has been involved with refugee crises across the world, including the Calais, France camp known as The Jungle, 2016

Below: In Izmir, Turkey, the Global Free Unit works with local partners to design and build new facilities for the large number of Syrian refugees trapped in the country following the EU-Turkey deal, 2017

With the increasing commodification of the students' experience, this mutual relationship has taken a turn. Education today is regarded as a substantial investment to be sustained by students themselves while academic institutions undertake aggressive building programs, commissioning iconic and hugely expensive urban facilities as a way of competing with one another in order to attract students at an international scale. All of this drives processes of gentrification or "studentification" within the major metropolises and feeds a growing sense of disillusionment towards the value of education, its economic viability, and its ethical stance. As a result, many now question the university's place within the city.[1]

Nowhere is this issue, being spatial in nature, more felt than in architecture. This became apparent while I was editing, alongside Harriet Harriss and Rory Hyde, the book *Architects After Architecture: Alternative Pathways for Practice* (Routledge, 2020), which traces the paths of those who, out of necessity or disillusionment, abandoned more conventional routes to architectural learning and practice to apply their skills and training to other fields, from tech to politics and art to the humanitarian sector. A case in point is the experience of Robert Mull, who set up the Global Free Unit (GFU), an itinerant organization that places architecture students from formal urban institutions into contexts of deprivation, displacement, and political uncertainty—be it a penitentiary in the UK or a refugee camp in Africa, Turkey, Greece, or France. The GFU addresses the prohibitive costs of education by providing free, fully accredited training, while also giving students the chance to work on real-life projects and channeling resources and expertise to communities in need of help.

Another example featured in the book is that of Shareen Elnaschie, who, after turning away from private architectural practice, was so struck by the experience and design talent among the refugee community on the Greek island of Lesbos, that she decided to establish the Office of Displaced Designers (ODD), an NGO that supports learning and professional opportunities for refugees in various design disciplines, helping people at their most vulnerable to reclaim their identity and self-worth.

Although these initiatives are still in their infancy, the pressures under which they have emerged are growing, and they call for new types of institutions that are more agile and less entrenched within a given set of buildings. Being placeless in this sense doesn't mean doing away with physical space, i.e., moving education entirely online. Much like the first placeless universities in the Middle Ages, ODD and the GFU are well-grounded within the realities within which they operate, yet their architectures, dynamism, and sense of purpose, rather than their buildings, are offering new paths forward in times of crisis.

[1] See Thomas Bender, *The University and the City: From Medieval Origins to the Present* (Oxford University Press, 1988).

In March 2020, we had two days to establish and run a food distribution operation in the London Borough of Lambeth that would be capable of delivering food and essentials to 6,000 residents who had to isolate due to their vulnerability to COVID-19. My role was to be the boots on the ground in setting up the operation. This involved the following:

1 – Identify, visit, and assess potential locations that we would use to receive, process, and distribute food and supplies.

2 – Bring sites up to code in terms of ramped access, hygiene, security, and operational layout, and equip them with everything needed to load and handle several tons of food in and out each day.

3 – Prepare floor plans to ensure that physical distancing is built into the operation.

4 – Run the operation for the first couple of days before handing over to a volunteer manager to take over from there.

5 – Move on to the next site, repeat.

We were relying on the network of primarily Council-owned buildings ranging from leisure centers, youth centers, schools, adventure playgrounds, and community halls to much smaller community rooms, flats, shop fronts, and garages. We had to deal with issues ranging from infestations, leaks, and structural roof issues to the need to quickly make wheelchair ramps, as almost all of the buildings predated equality legislation and had not been retrofitted. This was a unique moment to discover the community infrastructure in the borough as a whole and reflect on its condition. It was equally insightful to reflect on the challenges we experienced serving residents based on

the type of buildings in which they lived, from ground-level and mid-rise residences to high-rise properties either privately owned or Council-owned. Supporting this mix of housing and tenure types through one public service made the stark housing inequalities clear. For example, the high-rise Council blocks were the only locations that required paid staff to make deliveries. We couldn't use volunteers to service old high-rise buildings because of consistently broken lifts and entry systems, carrying distances, and safety concerns posed by travel through communal spaces with their many contact points.

When housing inequality directly affects your ability to support vulnerable people, you see, feel, and experience the seemingly small, mundane problems that accumulate to create serious daily issues. Most architecture students are aware that housing inequality exists in some form or other:

1 – High-density housing relies heavily on communal facilities to provide access to properties (corridors, lifts, stairs, security doors, concierge, etc.), facilities that are simply not necessary in properties with direct access to the street.

2 – The quality of communal facilities across the public- and private-sector housing provision varies immensely; it is worth interrogating the revenue model and incentives that influence how revenue is invested in these facilities.

3 – The absence and/or degradation of essential communal facilities in buildings as a result of reactive, slow, or under-invested maintenance models (e.g., broken lifts, leaks, stair access only) makes simple tasks challenging and increases the risk of exposure to public health threats, such as the coronavirus.

The questions and issues that I have been
reflecting on since, and the challenge I set to
students is to consider the following:

1 – Develop an awareness of the economic, moral,
and social incentives that influence decision
making in the built environment, decisions that lead
to the buildings we see around us.

2 – What are the incentives for spatial and housing
equality in a largely market-led development
sector?

3 – How can you use your understanding of
incentives to consider development models that
balance economic development incentives with the
more moral/social need for housing equality?

4 – What kind of development models will stand the
best chance of prioritizing equality at an impactful
scale?

Top: Lockdown food distribution operation in the London Borough of
Lambeth, 2020

One significant role of the state in the national
education systems of the world is to perpetuate
social and economic injustice.
—Colin Ward[1]

The Studio Symposium investigated sites of
learning in the contemporary city: Where do we
learn, what do we learn, who teaches and who
learns, what are the aims of that learning? At
present, our formal education structures, from
primary school to institutions of higher education,
reinforce power imbalances and other injustices
fostered and perpetuated by neoliberalism.

As a teacher and activist in the built environment, I
look for and advocate for new forms of participation
and agency in spatial practices to reestablish
the link between knowledge, power, and civic
life. My practice is driven by a loose collection
of ideas and tools that might inform our working
towards the idea of a co-produced city that is just
and sustainable. Anarchism is at the root of this.
So, let me introduce you to my anarchist hero,
Colin Ward. In 1984, he attended the International
Anarchist Gathering in Venice, sparked by George
Orwell's novel, *Nineteen Eighty-Four* (1949). At that
gathering, the focus was on:

. . . the role of insurgent place-making,
occupations of public space, and the role of
visible transformations of the built environment

in resistance, community organizing, and
experimentation in sustainable land use and
planning.

Over 35 years later, the importance of this approach
is more critical than ever, as the devastating
effects of neoliberalism are forcing and inspiring
more people and communities to take action,
creating pockets of resistance and people power.
Colin Ward was a prolific author and teacher
who advocated a type of quiet, sensible anarchy,
and in his many wonderful books he shared and
documented projects that placed people over
profit, celebrating their marvelous but often
marginal present with the desire to create a future
in which they were the norm, not the exception.
He championed things and people on the margins,
often hidden—community growers, self-builders,
council estate kids, rural squatters, et al.

Colin theorized moments of "pragmatist
anarchism" that removed authoritarian forms of
organization and governance in favor of informal
and self-organized mechanisms based on non-
hierarchical structures. The key principles of his
anarchism were mutual aid, self-organization, and

[1] Colin Ward, "The Role of the State" in *Education Without Schools*,
P. Buckman, ed. (London: Souvenir Press, 1973), 39–48

collective action, with respect for nature and each other versus capitalist ideals of self-interest, greed, and competition.

Today we can feel overwhelmed by all the injustice and inequality in our cities, the climate crisis, threats to democracy, etc. It seems that those at the top—the one percent—are somehow still clinging to power. In the face of this crushing reality, I look for places of informal learning where anarchist thinking and action can be found: in contemporary society—wikis, open-source software, the expanding co-operative movement, tenants' associations, trade unions, mutual aid groups, informal support networks; in architecture and urbanism—self-build, co-housing, community energy companies, Community Land Trusts, city farms and kitchens, community centers, neighborhood plans, Libraries of Things. As Colin explained in his book, *Anarchy in Action* (1973):

An anarchist society, a society that organizes itself without authority, is always in existence, like a seed beneath the snow.

Thank you, Colin. I will keep looking and learning.

Top: Alicia's collection of Colin Ward books.

We tend to think of sites of learning as aesthetically, programmatically, and even spatially divorced from our everyday lives. Academia is frequently likened to an ivory tower; vocational studies seem increasingly confined to a world of impenetrable acronyms, from CIMAs (Chartered Institute of Management Accountants), to NVQs (National Vocational Qualification), to ARBs (Architects Registration Board); and even the admirable aim of "continuing professional development" brings to mind specialized spaces and specified occasions that are somewhat outside the usual ebb and flow of emails, Zoom calls, and emails during Zoom calls.

In acknowledgement of this, much of our work with the RESOLVE Collective is centered around a design philosophy we call "using the site as a resource," which for us means working both with local, everyday materials and local, everyday knowledge—using these to rethink how and where we learn through practice. We understand the "site" not just as the demarcation of our professional remit, but also as part of a constellation of everyday spaces within which we must actively position ourselves. As such, learning with and from the site becomes a necessary exercise in "situatedness", whereby design is socialized and spatial practice accumulates with location, existing in constant dialogue with a variety of tacit, disparate knowledge.

Using a selection of four of our past projects, we have attempted to elucidate how our practice has been significantly shaped by everyday sites of learning.

Left: *Programming Im/Passivity*, Braunschweig, Germany installation, 2020, RESOLVE Collective

The Garage, Sheffield: Learning from the City

The Garage was an artist residency in S1 Artspace, Sheffield, situated in the old garage of the famous Park Hill Estate undergoing redevelopment by Urban Splash. The project was inspired by conversations that had occupied us internally around how people's realities differ, even in the same neighborhood or city, and also the work of urban planner Kevin Lynch, which we drew on and augmented heavily throughout the project. Working with a variety of groups across Sheffield, from poets like Otis Mensah and Warda Yassin to community groups such as the Manor & Castle Residents Association and local schools, we created an installation and two-month public program that interrogated people's emotional responses to their built environment.

Our site for this project was the network of art spaces across the city from which we reused materials for the installation. However, this became in many ways an entry point to the city as a site of learning; we drew on awe-inspiring networks of young creatives and initiatives that wove through the city and were fueled by their complex narratives of labor, migration, and familial connection. Valuing these networks through a practice of "platforming" became more important than ever for this project, as we were gripped by the urgency of making space for critically overlooked creative practitioners in our cities.

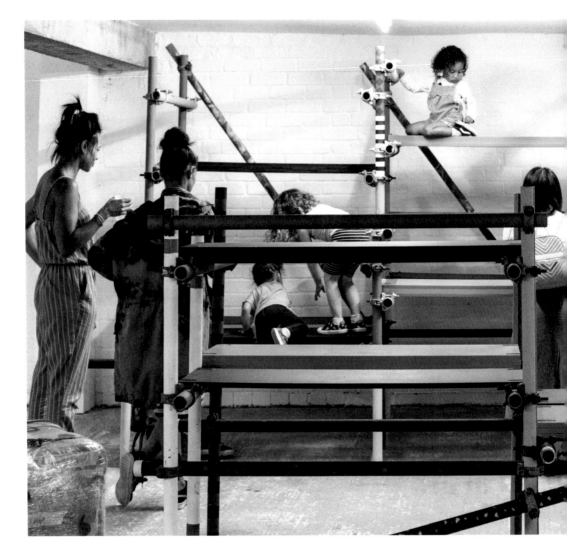

Playing Pretend, Hull: Learning from the Learners

"Playing Pretend" was a syllabus workshop series delivered with registered charity Absolutely Cultured in Hull for students from three primary schools located across the city. With the young designers, we looked at how by "playing pretend" we might imagine magical, hopeful, and even radical urban futures. Each workshop investigated one of five urban themes: Transport, Health, High Streets, Maintenance and Care, and City Design. Within each theme, we challenged our junior design team to address current problems, imagine future solutions, and bring their interventions to life through drawing, model-making, role playing, clay sculpture, and a number of other creative practices. The workshops culminated in a temporary space in Hull's city center that spatialized the workshop process, opening it up to children from across the city.

Tapping into this dynamic space of memory, play, and perception allowed us to think critically about how we design for young people, not only spatially but programmatically. We worked to the rhythms of a young person's city, rather than one defined by professional silos, and were consequently pushed to reprioritize and unlearn certain rigidities in our approach, from the hard-won realization of how to sensitively facilitate silent and noisy work to working harder to value messy processes over more well-curated objects.

Top: The Garage, Sheffield S1 Art Gallery Residency, London 2019, RESOLVE Collective

Our "site" in this project wasn't the gallery but instead a network of socio-historical spaces of Black diasporic identity in Europe. We navigated textual space and physical space with a similar remit, actively (or impassively) using our own identities as a means of cohering archival fragments and material lives. We learned in a traditional way, gaining insight into a world we had been painfully unaware of, but we also learned through the practice of having to position ourselves within past lives. We have since held the notion of "life" within an archive dear to our design approach.

Close From Afar, London: Learning from the Site

Close From Afar was an installation and public program with NOW Gallery in London and a group of amazing student volunteers from the University of Greenwich. This project looked at the idea of the "global" as a proliferation of "locals," seeking to illuminate and celebrate the strength of local capital, community resilience, and decentralized organization in our societies. The public program drew on the work of local organizations in the surrounding areas of the Greenwich Peninsula on both sides of the Thames, from Woolwich to Limehouse. The installation design was comprised solely of waste materials we salvaged from the adjacent site of the Design District, reflecting the almost respiratory-like nature of material availability on the construction site: designing with abundance when it exhaled brick off-cuts, tarmac, Styrofoam, and oriented strand board, but designing with scarcity when it contracted, eventually integrating our site workshop. The site—with the variety of nearby local neighborhoods and the area dedicated for construction on the peninsula—gave us an invaluable opportunity to interrogate the connection, and often disconnection, between local lives and the processes of urban development. We learned of the powerfully associative quality that many everyday materials have for local people—far beyond their structural significance or design intention—and have since sought to center the attempt to bring out this quality in the found materials of our projects as part of our core design methodology.

Programming Im/Passivity, Braunschweig: Learning from Reflection

Programming Im/Passivity was a three-part project with the Kunstverein Braunschweig in Braunschweig, Germany that looked at the life of the eighteenth-century Ghanaian-German philosopher, Anton Wihelm Amo. The parts consisted of a "curatorial sphere" in which we sought to exhibit and disseminate the work of Amo and our research into his life and practice; a "programmatic sphere" in which participants were invited to delve into his work; and a "spatial sphere" in which, working with a local school, we transformed a gallery space using material techniques that were interpreted from his various philosophical treatises.

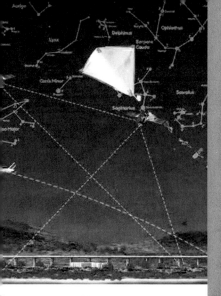

Studio Research

The studio began with a series of research exercises, where students explored their personal geographies and conducted precedent analysis of alternative learning models, which included:

- Task 1: Triptychs

- Task 2: Yale Spatial Analysis

- Task 3: Alternative Learning Models and Sites

Left: Vignesh Harikrishnan, based in Chennai, India

Task 1: Triptychs

Each student analyzed their personal geography
during lockdown, and interrogated the spatial and
network implications of post-COVID learning. Their
analysis led them to potential sites and a sense
of what their particular alternative learning model
was in relation to their physical lockdown setting.
For the deliverable, students produced a triptych
capturing thoughts and observations at three
scales—personal, territorial, and network—through
hand-drawn and digital drawing-collage-diagrams.
As opposed to finished pieces, these outputs were
working tools used to open up possibilities and
identify latent spatial relationships.

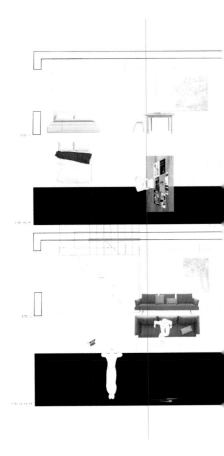

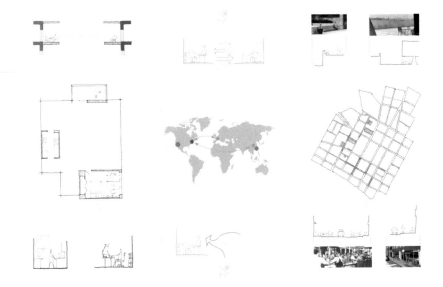

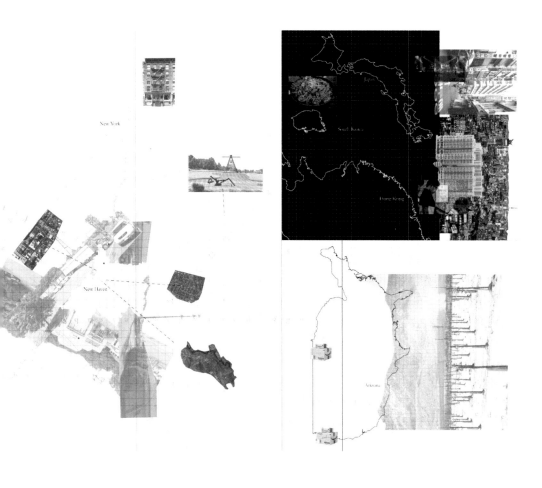

Left: Justin Kong, based in Hong Kong   Top: Shuang Chen, based in China

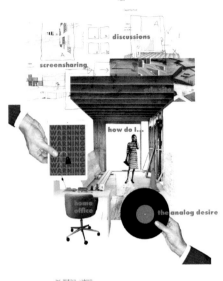

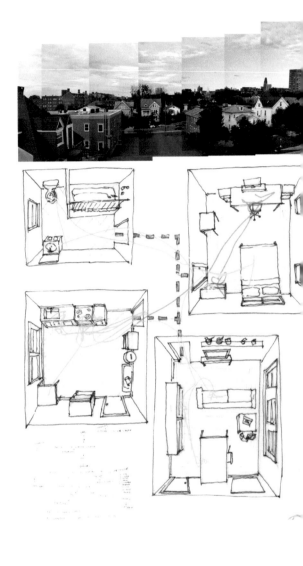

Left: Saba Salekfard, based in Los Angeles, CA

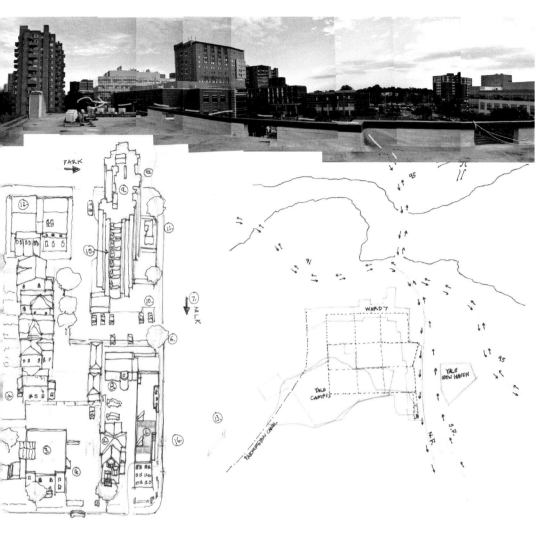

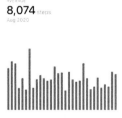

AVERAGE
8,074 steps
Aug 2020

Top: Ben Thompson, based in New Haven, CT

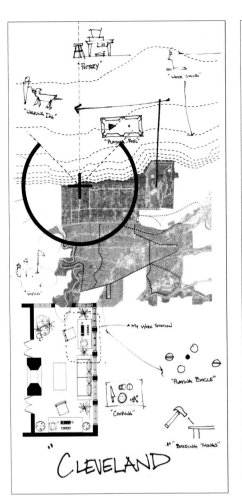

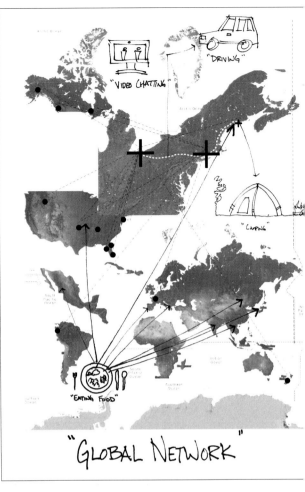

Top: Tyler Krebs, based in New Haven, CT and Cleveland, OH

Right: Saba Salekfard, based in Los Angeles, CA

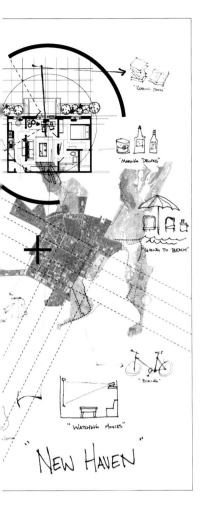

"READING BOOKS"

"MAKING DRINKS"

"GOING TO BEACH"

"BIKING"

"WATCHING MOVIES"

"NEW HAVEN"

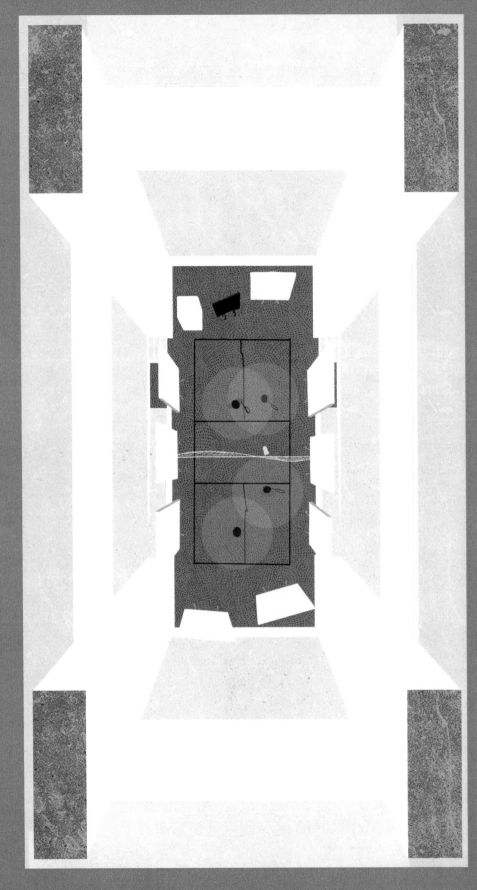

Task 2: Yale Spatial Analysis

In groups of three, students analyzed the spatial conditions of Yale, looking beyond the immediate situation to reveal the layers of interrelationships derived from or influencing the spatial relationships of YSoA, both from the point of view of private individuals as well as a variety of publics, or groups of people with differing concerns. Those include:

• Nature: resources used, generated, threats to the natural environment

• Culture: social origins of education, forms of association and architectures, etc.

• Infrastructure: mobility, energy, health, security

• Governance: who runs it and what are the rules and rights

• Commerce: the knowledge economy, the financial model for education from a student's POV

• Fashion: what's in, what's out, what are the short-term influences and trends versus the long-term disruptions

The resulting work was presented as plans, maps, and diagrams that analyzed relevant aspects.

Left: Rudolph Hall Fourth-Floor Pit as a badminton court, Claudia Ansorena

Architectural and Personal Scale

Rudolph Hall's Fourth Floor Pit

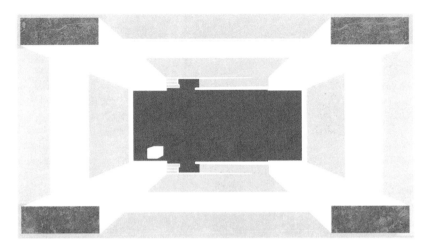

On a regular day

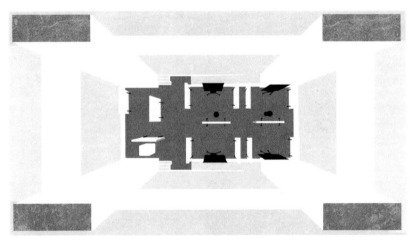

As a classroom space on a block-schedule

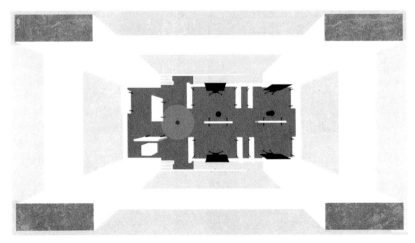

During the time of social distancing

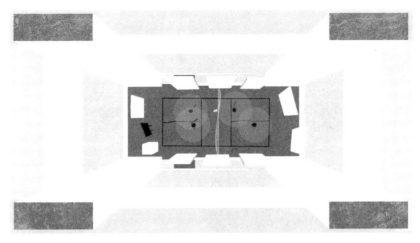

As a badminton court

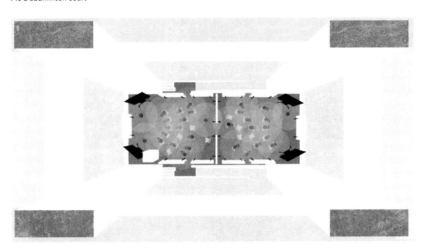

As a space for pinups, reviews, and presentations

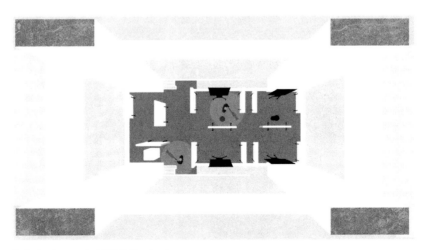

Daily cleaning as part of COVID-19 protocol

Urban, Neighborhood, and City Scale

New Haven, CT

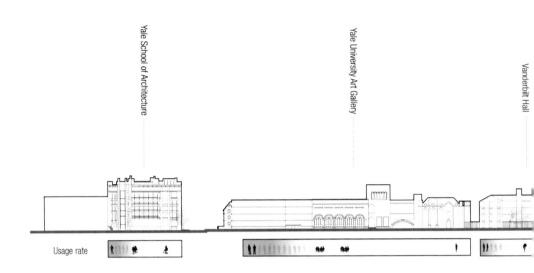

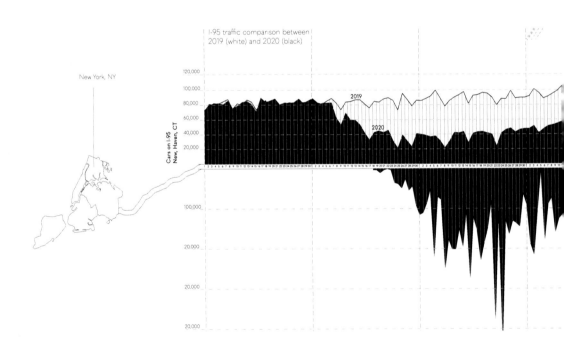

Top: COVID-19 and its relationship to civic life on Chapel Street,
New Haven, Gordan Jiang

Bottom: COVID-19 and its relationship to traffic on I-95,
Tyler Krebs

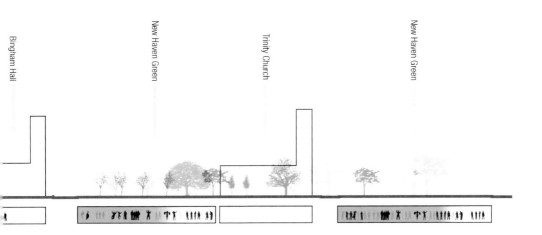

Bingham Hall

New Haven Green

Trinity Church

New Haven Green

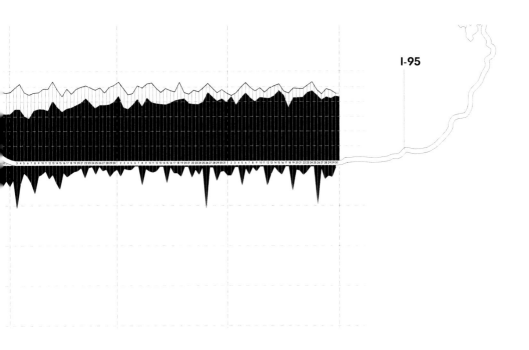

I-95

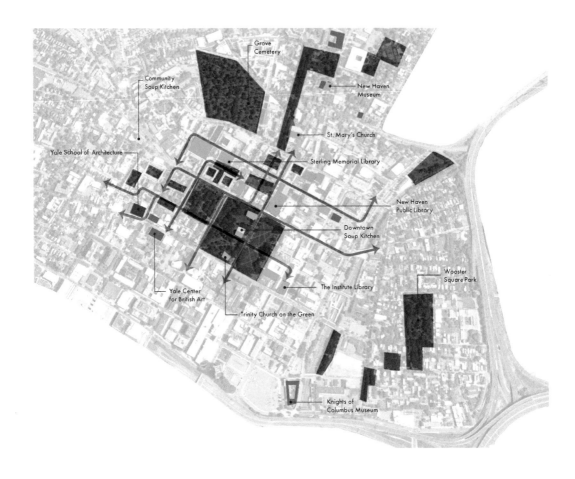

Grove
Cemetery

Community
Soup Kitchen

New Haven
Museum

St. Mary's Church

Yale School of Architecture

Sterling Memorial Library

New Haven
Public Library

Downtown
Soup Kitchen

Wooster
Square Park

Yale Center
for British Art

The Institute Library

Trinity Church on the Green

Knights of
Columbus Museum

Top: New Haven public programs and pedestrian networks,
Saba Salekfard

Top: New Haven public parks and transportation routes,
Saba Salekfard

Network and Global Scale

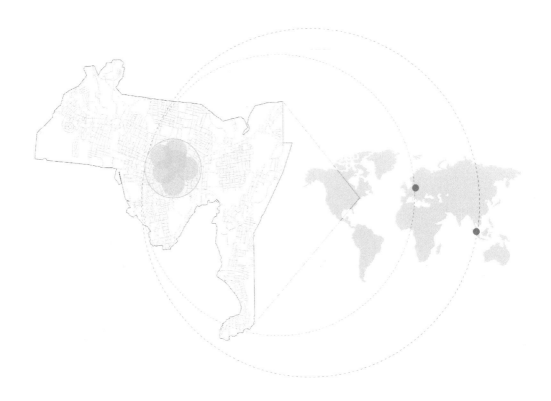

Right: Yale University's Global Network Pre-Pandemic, where most students were concentrated in the city of New Haven, Ashton Harrell

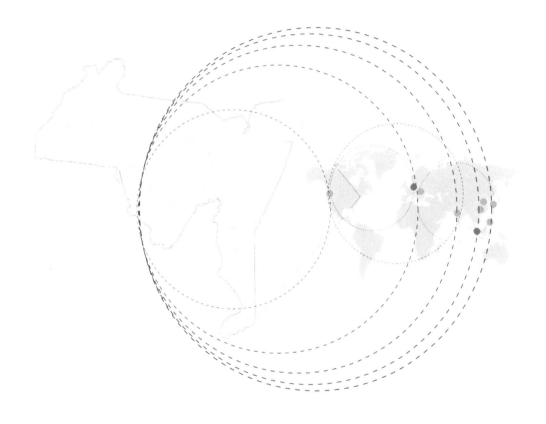

Top: Yale University's Global Network Post-Pandemic, where
students dispersed amongst locations throughout the US, India, and
China, Ashton Harrell

Guidalpina

Lemonade Day

Breakthru

GEN Austin

For the City Network

Acton Children's Business
Fair

Social Profit Village

Pet

Acton Academy

Sustainable Food

Acton Business School

Found

Discover HI

Cooking Up Cultures

Skillpoint Alliance

University of Texas College
of Liberal Arts

DLA Piper

DLA Piper NEST

Economic Growth Busini
Incubator

Lumbra Ventures

ScribeS

in.
in.gredients

Filament Labs

Top: Map of the networks of various Yale partners,
Vignesh Harikrishnan

Southwest Key Programs

Patient Planning Services

EDCO Ventures

Solar Texas Investment Club · Slow Food Austin

Austin Foodshed Investors

Vuka

EcoRise

Avnide

well aware
Well Aware

TEDMED Austin

Impact Texas · Whole Foods Market · Save Money Austin

Seton Healthcare Family

Blue Avocado

Innovations Plus Social Good

Livestrong Foundation

tor\

MentorWings

Conscious Capitalism Austin

Summer of Hope · Mentergram

Digital Union

CenterSt

Austin Center for Design

SXSW Interactive

Raven + Lily

Puente Phone

Vo'
ThinkVoting

Ten Acre Organics · Girl Guild

Tech Ranch

Whole Planet Foundation

ATX Hack 4 Change

CTC International

Austin Plus Social Good

Yarb

Social Velocity · Charity Charge

Paradox Capital

Entrepreneurs Foundation of Central Texas · College Forward

Multicultural Refugee Coalition: Open Arms

Aunt Bertha

Greenling

UHEM USA

Stretch Recipes · LBJ School of Public Affairs

Build A Sign.com

RGK Center

Owen's Garage

Core Media

Texas Venture Labs Accelerator · Austin Bicycle

Incubator

St. Edward's University

GiveLights · Caphouse Policy

Philanthropitch

University of Texas

Compost Pedallers

Capital Factory

RGK Foundation

United Way

Colin's Hope · Explore Austin

USED)

Fusebox · Easter Seals

Caritas · WeVива · SVDP Diocese

Mother's Milk Bank

Combs School of Business

ALL · Third Sector Partners

E3 Alliance

Task 3, Part I: Alternative Learning Models and Sites

This exercise consisted of precedent analysis of alternative learning models, including: YSoA; Rural Studio (Johannesburg); London School of Architecture; Open University; University of the Underground; and alternative models selected by the students.

University of the Underground

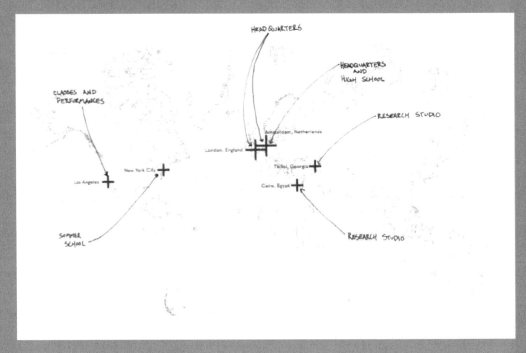

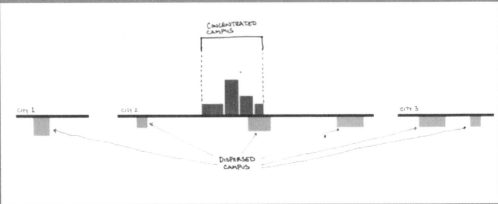

Top: Networks and campus locations of the University of the Underground, Tyler Krebs

Bottom: Dispersed campus model of the University of the Underground, Tyler Krebs

Rural Studio

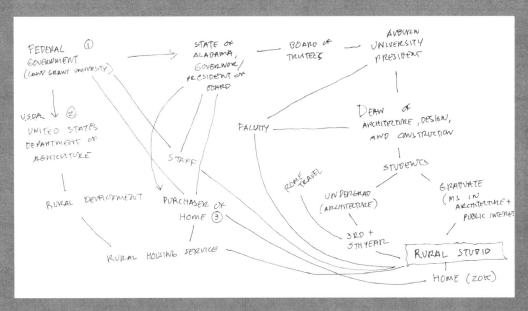

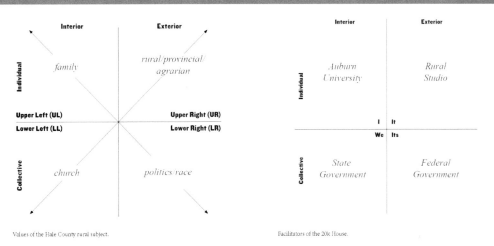

Values of the Hale County rural subject.

Facilitators of the 20k House.

Top: Organizational diagram of Rural Studio, Ben Thompson

Bottom: Integral theory diagram of Rural Studio, Ben Thompson

Task 3, Part II: Final Project Site Selection

Each student selected the site for learning and speculated on an alternative learning model for their individual projects.

Claudia Ansorena
Miami, FL

How do architects design for unknown futures while simultaneously engaging the challenges of their time? The architecture student should be taught to exist and design in various time zones—i.e., the past, the present, the future—in order to best frame their role in ever-changing societies. Relying on memory, observation, and data as tools for learning, this alternate model situated in Miami, Florida seeks to provide architects with hands-on learning from an interdisciplinary perspective, including four key actors responsible for changes in the built environment: government, community, designers, and researchers. Thus, the site and subsequent building postulate a future Miami that, although physically changed by the vestiges of nature, becomes a laboratory of knowledge, cross-pollination, and action for the betterment of place.

Right: Proposed Miami River site location

Shuang Chen
New York, NY

MoMA PS1 and the Sculpture Center are both located in Hunters Point, Long Island City, Queens, a lively artists' hub with a long industrial history. However, due to the gentrification process, artists and art studios have vanished from this area. The building, for instance, used to house three hundred artists, and its facade served as a renowned canvas for graffiti art. It was demolished in 2019 when the owner developed condominiums. Although there are many museums and galleries in Long Island City, artists' spaces and studios are rapidly disappearing. I intend to build up a patchwork of art studio spaces to resurrect the cultural creativity of the area by identifying and utilizing abandoned factories and vacant lots.

Right: Site image collage

Ashton Harrell
New York, NY

In past years, the rapid growth of the academic machine with its ballooning cost has mirrored the billions in student loan debt and cemented the rise of inaccessible, centralized university models. Architecture, education, and urbanism battle over space and resources as campuses face the challenges of navigating the social, spatial, and architectural conditions of the urban environment. Urban schools play an important role in shaping cities. However, can cities instead play a role in redeveloping the built campus and revisioning educational models, freeing the wandering scholar from the constraints of the academic building? In evolutionary ecology, parasitism is the symbiotic relationship between species wherein one organism, the parasite, lives on or in another organism, the host. This field of research examines universities and schools as the parasite that establishes a symbiotic relationship to the academic community, as a site of pedagogical transformation. This project analyzes New York City as a host site.

Right: Proposed site options for interventions

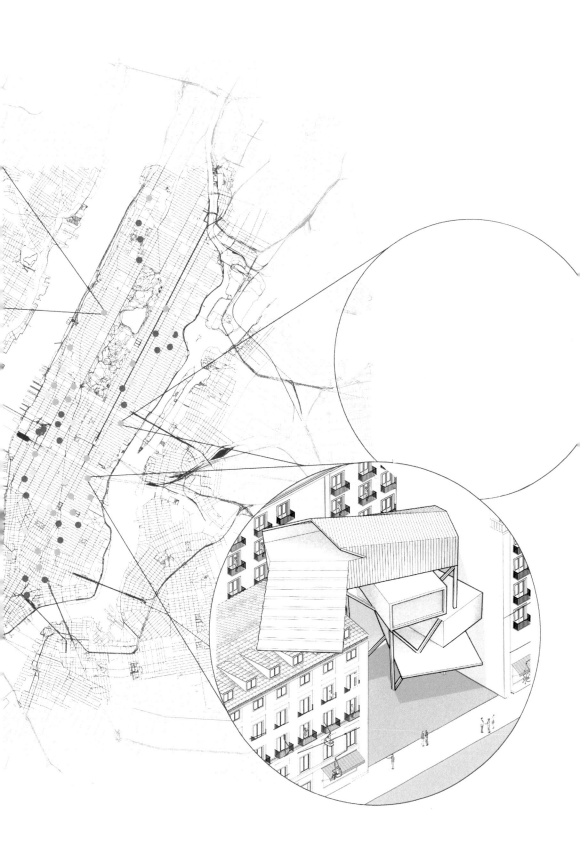

Justin Kong
Hong Kong, China

Minuscule and dense, Hong Kong is a place of hyperconnectivity. Yet, the experience of learning, which is hyper-siloed from the general public, has suggested otherwise. In confronting this discrepancy, a spatial network of collaboration and shared space that takes advantage of the existing infrastructure system is imagined for the current educational landscape, which consists of eight universities. In establishing their presence at the heart of the city and in acting together, the learning experience they offer would not be limited to enrolled students. The general public, which is spatially disenfranchised, would be able to engage and contribute to the built environment.

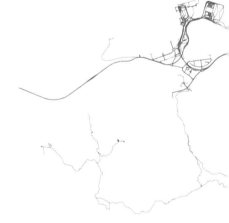

Right: Potential sites and existing university campuses

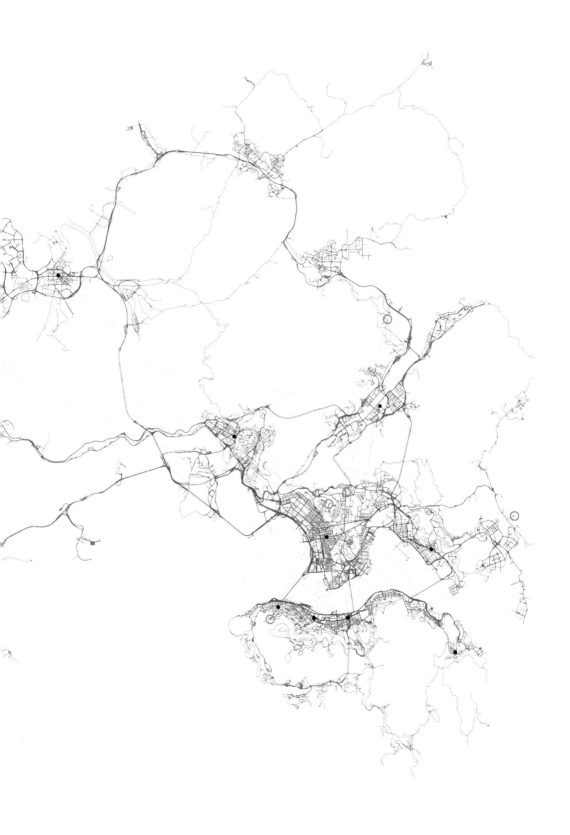

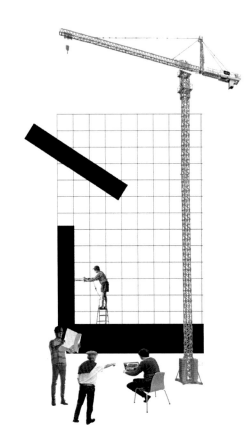

Tyler Krebs
Cleveland, OH

Extreme poverty, segregation, scant resources, and lack of community engagement have given Cleveland, Ohio the distinction of having one of the nation's worst public-school systems. The area's community groups believe that neighborhoods desperately need well-designed and effectively stewarded spaces where residents can gather across class, ethnic, racial, geographic and generational divides. My proposal is to create a design school whose curriculum is rooted in the creation of an annual cultural event. This event will bring together disparate peoples while its infrastructure will be shared with local schools and adapt to fit their needs. Most importantly, students participating in the program will gain real-world experience in making their community better.

Top: "Event" as intervention collage for Cleveland

Saba Salekfard
Los Angeles, CA

The misfits of architecture seek to disrupt the
formalized structure of academia. They advocate
for an organic development of learning through
physical explorations of place and informal
situations. The project will use famous cultural
monuments of Los Angeles, such as the Hollywood
Sign or Walt Disney Concert Hall, as sites for
interventions. Failures, process, and in-progress
works are the drivers behind the project's
architectural strategy. Exploring the boundaries
of the sacred and the profane, the misfits aim to
deconstruct the "worship culture" of architecture
and give work back to the greater community.

Right: "Misfits of Architecture" monument intervention collage

CLOSED

OPEN

OPEN

CLOSED

CLOSED

CLOSED

CLOSED

OPEN

OPEN

CLOSED
RAZED

CLOSED

Ben Thompson
Oakland, MI

Education and consumerism have assumed
opposite trajectories. The shopping mall and
big-box store's dense nodes have given way to
online shopping and delivery. Meanwhile, the old
model of public secondary schools embedded
in neighborhoods has disappeared as districts
have chosen to consolidate into large, centralized
educational complexes. These former school sites
in Oakland, Michigan have been razed for public
parks, residential infill, or sold for commercial
development. The shopping centers, with their
steel-framed skeletons and open floor plans, have
a strong adaptive reuse potential as sites of almost
infinitely malleable forms of education that should
be considered.

Top: Potential site options map

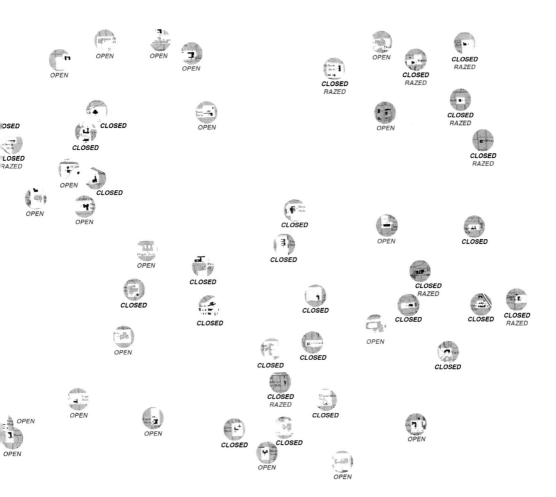

Student Work

Learning from Precarity

Claudia Ansorena

Given the speculative and theoretical frameworks that ultimately disillusion recent architecture school graduates, how can students of architecture become better prepared to design for the unknown while simultaneously engaging with the challenges of their time?

The architecture student should be taught to exist and design in various time zones—that is, the past, the present, the future—in order to frame their role in ever-changing societies. Relying on memory, observation, and data as tools for learning, this alternate model provides architects-to-be with hands-on experience from an interdisciplinary perspective.

Four key actors—government agencies, community leaders, designers, and researchers—will help realize intervention-based attachments to the existing infrastructure of Miami and introduce new typologies that will be integral to the survival of our cities. Situating itself in a near future of a drastic sea-level rise and seasonal coastal flooding, the project envisions a possible reality wherein Miami becomes a host to climate adaptation experimentation and agile learning in precarity.

Top: View from the houseboat village

Right: Site plan with proposed highway street typology

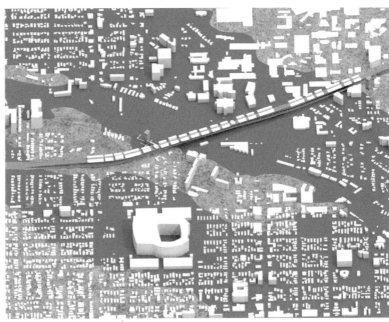

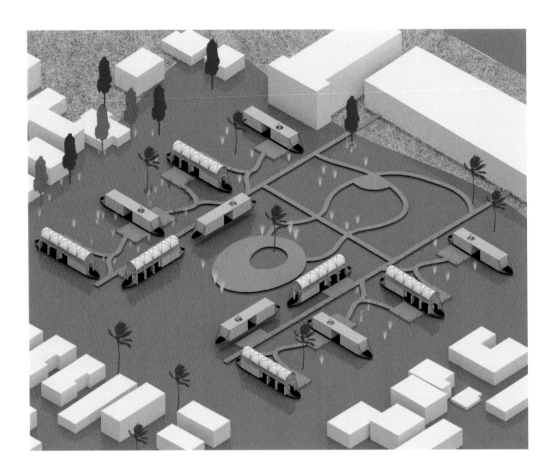

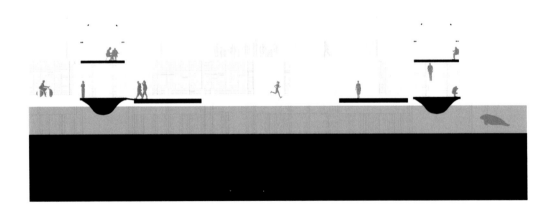

Top: Aerial view of houseboat village typology   Bottom: Section of houseboat village

Top: Aerial view of tower typology

Bottom right: Aerial view of floating garden typology

Bottom left: Aerial view of highway street typology

Next page: Section through tower typology

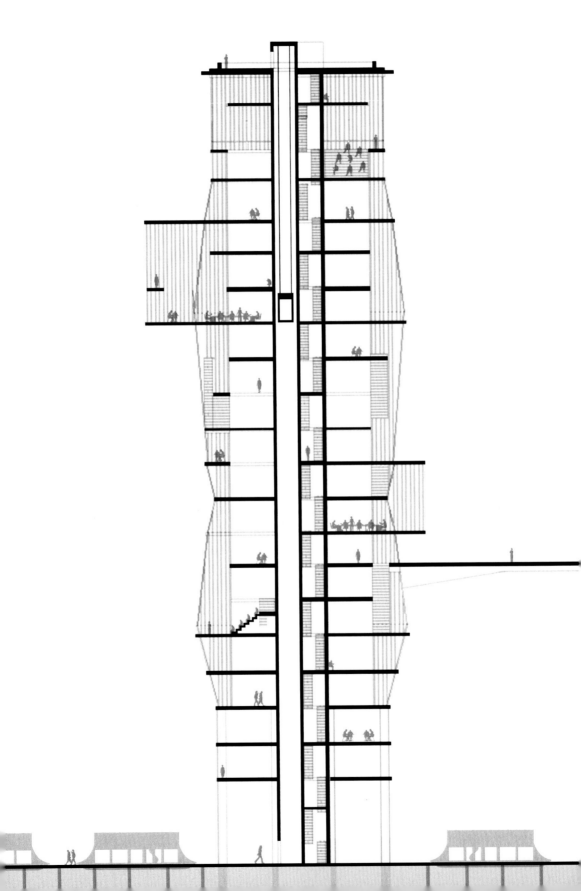

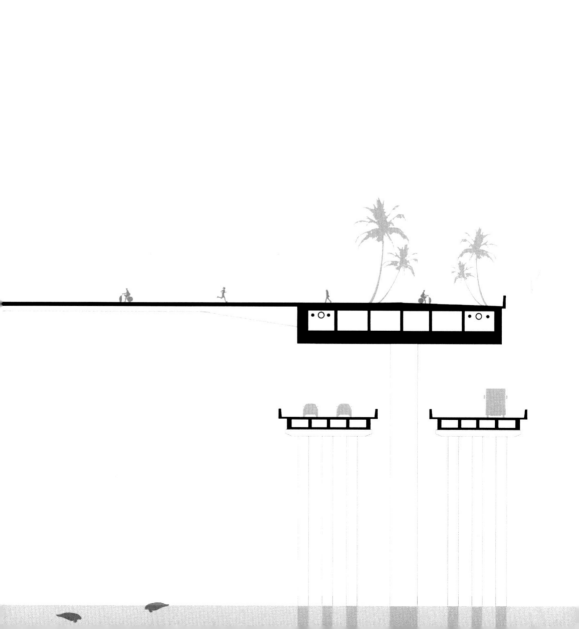

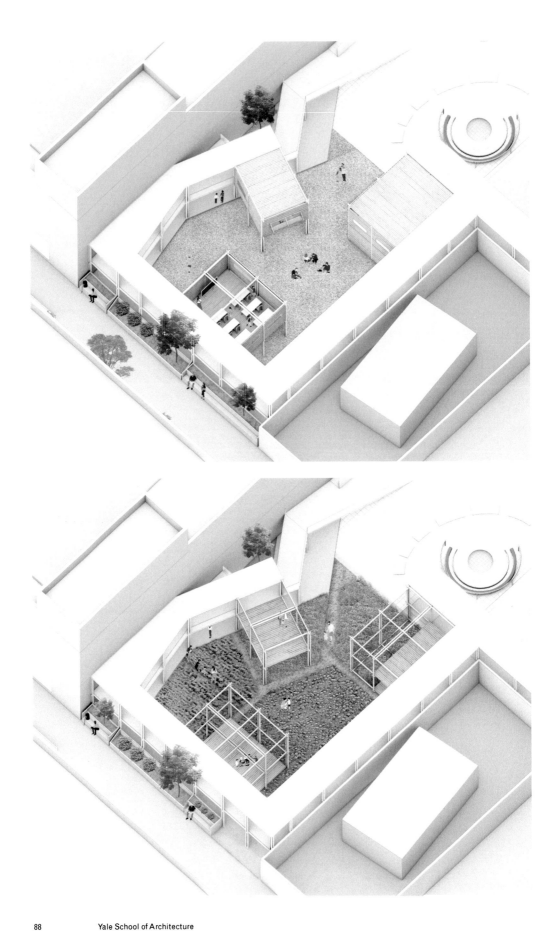

The City Campus

Shuang Chen

The City Campus project aims to provide a new outdoor learning experience in Hunters Point as an extended campus. Hunters Point was a former industrial hub with factories such as Pepsi-Cola, Eagle Electric, and Plaxall. However, since 2001, the neighborhood was rezoned into mixed-use and residential, which encouraged factory owners to sell to the highest bidder. The area has experienced substantial commercial and residential growth, especially along the waterfront and around the Court Square transit hub. The Hunters Point population has, in fact, increased by more than 20,000 in the past ten years. Due to the gentrification process, 10,000 new housing units were completed in 2020, but local infrastructure could not meet the demand. There are, nevertheless, a series of "leftover" spaces in this area, such as abandoned infrastructure, vacant lots, underpass spaces, and underutilized green space, that demonstrate the potential for active, occupiable open spaces.

The City Campus project proposed an alternative to the default mode of massive development, which comes with many challenges. The proposal: development plans with affordable housing units and pocket parks located no more than a quarter mile away, equal opportunities for education, and funding necessary to develop shared resources. In this new planning model, collaboration is critical. It has to take place between community groups, the New York City Department of Parks and Recreation, local arts and cultural institutions, and others. A new tour route will connect the leftover sites with existing cultural assets, parks, and sports amenities, and activities will be proposed for each site. Two sites will have a design that illustrates and embodies this citizen-learning idea. In this framework, everyone gets to own a piece of the learning resources, the neighborhood, and Hunters Point as a City Campus.

Top: Infill lot school site with additional playground

Left: Infill lot school site and growth over time

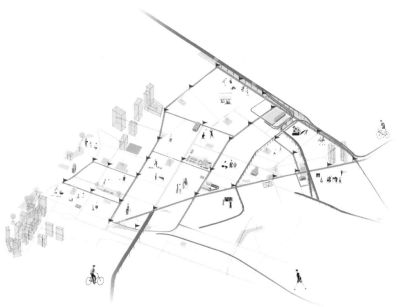

Top: Perspective view of the art and sports site

Bottom: Citizen learning framework diagram featuring new development, leftover "shadow" sites, cultural and art assets, park and sport amenities, and proposed bike routes

Top: Perspective view of art and sports site

Top: Perspective view of the art and sports site

Top right: Aerial view of art and sports site

Right: Alternative new deal diagram featuring "packages" : affordable housing units, equivalent school opportunities, pocket parks in 1/4-mile range, outdoor learning resources

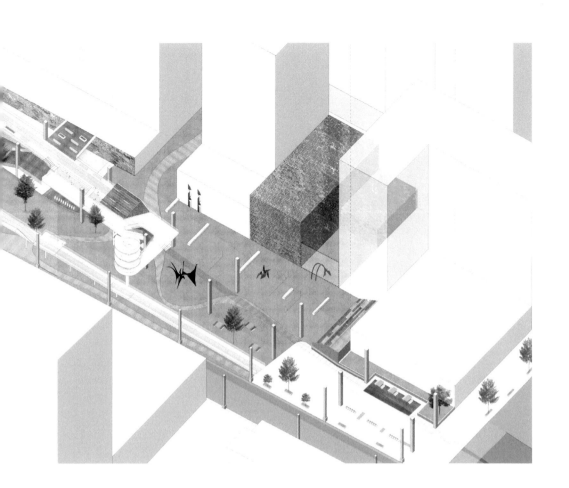

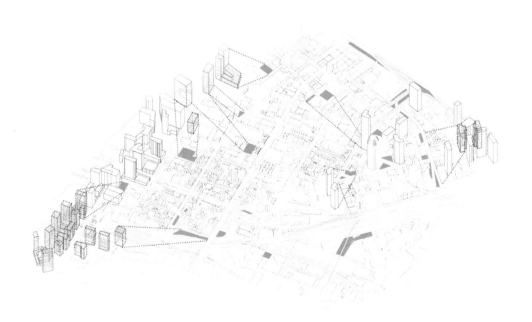

The Parasite

Ashton Harrell

Urbanism offers many non-functioning and unutilized resources and sites for consumption that would allow architects, artists, and even skilled laborers like mechanics and farmers to harvest immense riches from viewing and using the city as a campus. Traditional buildings for design schools and studios oblige users to fall into established hierarchical norms of use and learning. What if these models, focused on resources that can be mined from decaying sites rather than pumping external resources into them, could be decentralized and integrated throughout the city like Cedric Price's Thinkbelt critique of the traditional university system? Like parasites, they could extract vital aspects of traditional educational models and the urban lifecycle to engender small, flexible, highly specialized architecture that would support novel modes of learning and engagement between creators and the city. They would use architecture to convert sites of industrial production into sites for the production of knowledge.

Feeding off the city, The Parasitic School infests the urban landscape with creative experimentation and exhibition. Presenting as a chain of diverse spaces that crosses Manhattan from the Hudson River to the East River, the school attaches to the city's derelict infrastructure to define a new paradigm for learning, experimentation, and display. This free communal and social environment includes housing, study spaces, and exhibition and performance areas.

Right: Process collage of parasite architecture elements and techniques, based on Cedric Price's fun palace

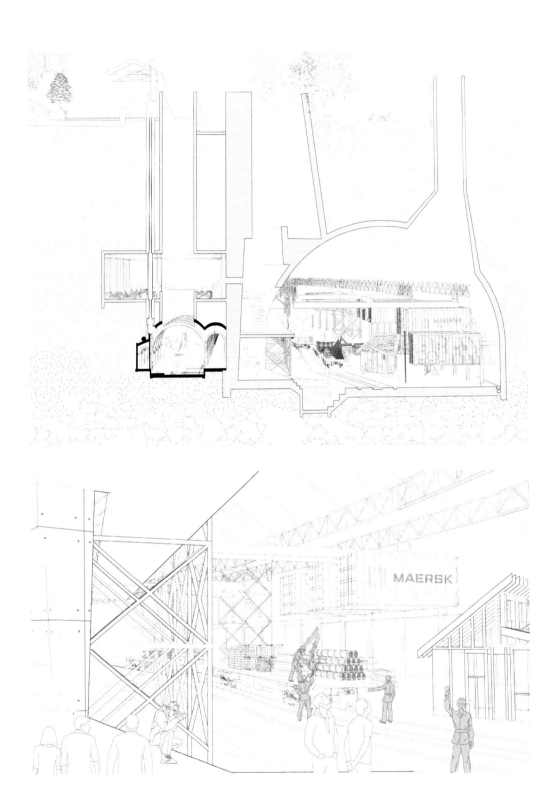

Top: Section cut of laboratory intervention   Bottom: Perspective view of laboratory site

Top: Section cut of quarry intervention   Bottom: Perspective view of quarry site

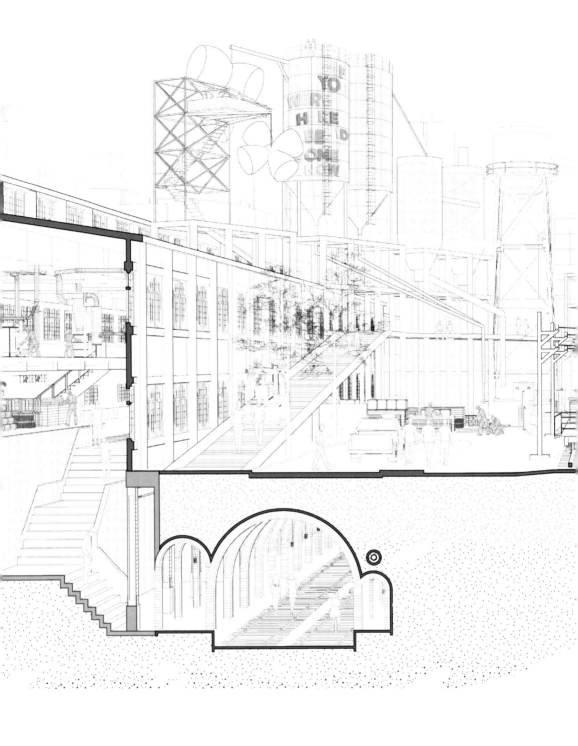

Top: Section of depot intervention

கோடை

KODAI

t Loopy

e circular economy through enga-
sign-and-make tasks, focusing on
sses, specifically, the circular economy principle that waste = food.

the opportunity to consider mass
or festival that they may be aware
he concept that if food packaging
rative instead of polluting. Conse-
on that lost packaging litter is da-
food packaging as nourishing the
astonbury music festival's theme
ut what if we left a positive mark
hat was left behind benefited the
further within different subjects:

food products suitable for selling
ckaging composting process, bio-
and the current use of polymers.

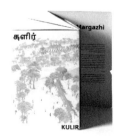

களிர்   Margazhi

KULIR

The Common Canal

Vignesh Harikrishnan

The Indian government's sudden enforcement of the COVID-19 lockdown, following a 14-hour Janata curfew on March 22, 2020, immediately disadvantaged already vulnerable populations as it restricted people from leaving their homes. Those caught away from home had problems returning. With road and rail transport links suspended, walking was the only option, and people took to the road on foot. Images of marching migrant workers showed them trying to return to their homes to reunite with their families. People undertook hazardous journeys, sometimes walking up to 1,000 kilometers with no money or food. Many were arrested by law enforcement officials for violating the lockdown, while some died due to exhaustion or accidents.

The notion of being vulnerable and displaced limits access to education. Buckingham Canal is the most polluted of the three major waterways in Janata. Our survey group met spatial and education injustices head-on by asking locals of the area if collective planning could enable access to learning for all, including displaced communities. We broached this issue in three phases. Surveying the inhabitants of Buckingham Canal using social media apps and the Yale Qualtrics Survey App led us to some answers, but questions also arose about the need for a shared collective. The project builds a case for collective planning as a means to give agency to inhabitants to reshape their environment by addressing spatial and educational injustice, as well as the climate crisis.

Left: "Orrery – the Mediums": Spatial and education injustices are met head on by asking if collective planning can address not only the climate crisis but enable access to learning for all, including displaced communities.

Further discussions with stakeholders, activists, educators, and politicians helped us to discuss a holistic framework of commons where learning and personal and social empowerment can coexist.

The discussions led to designing the underused institutional open spaces to maintain commons for reconstituting public control. The newly designed urban area will host a series of community-powered banking, learning hubs, and climate labs that will reaffirm the educational imperative. The learning model for children will be designed based on geography, politics, and economy, emphasizing the need for these disparate strands to come together. The Temporal Education Curriculum, which is based on seasonality, will anchor the context for children to associate with and belong to their place.

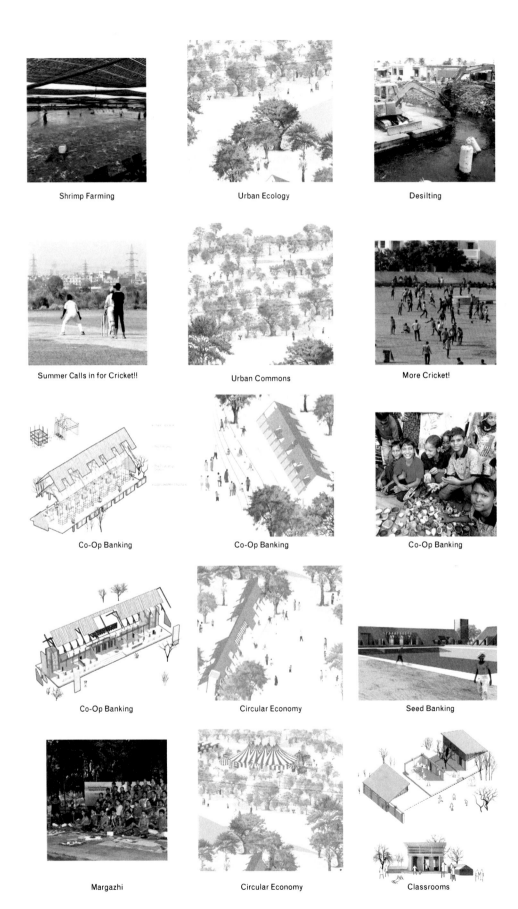

Shrimp Farming

Urban Ecology

Desilting

Summer Calls in for Cricket!!

Urban Commons

More Cricket!

Co-Op Banking

Co-Op Banking

Co-Op Banking

Co-Op Banking

Circular Economy

Seed Banking

Margazhi

Circular Economy

Classrooms

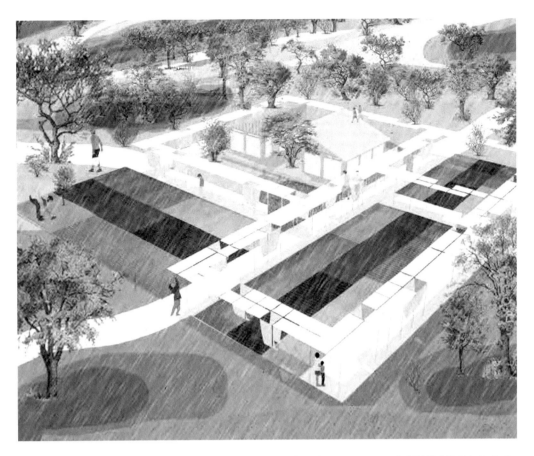

Left: Diagrams for an introduction to a circular economy, an urban ecology, and an urban commons.

Bottom Left: The wetlands are a highly programmed, linear sponge park, which would absorb the excess rain water and further release it to the ground and the canal.

Top: A barren land is chosen and the service corridors are deployed to demarcate the fields. The fabric corridor allows light and water to filter through the material and doubles up as a site for people to rest, eat, and sell products.

Bottom Right: Shelter housing is an integrral urban development process, building housing communities and citizens.

Left: This activity introduces aspects of the circular economy through engaging students with accessible design-and-make tasks, focusing on food packaging for festivals. It addresses, specifically, the circular economy principle that waste equals energy.

Center: A series of public parks, along with the re-zoned institutional playgrounds, can be reconstructed into wetlands in the event of flooding.

Right: Co-operative banks play a crucial role in financing, with funding of areas under agriculture, livestock, milk, personal finance, and
self-employment, and help setup small-scale units among the few
focus points for both urban and rural cooperative banks.

Hong Kong City Museum

Justin Kong

The idea of confinement in our traditional learning model preceded the pandemic, when there was already a disconnect from what we learn in the classroom and the city in which it is located. Referencing the alternative learning model implemented at the Graduate School of Architecture at the University of Johannesburg, I propose to introduce a dispersed learning network at Central Hong Kong University that emphasizes kinetic learning as part of an effort to capture and preserve the historic neighborhood's social vitality. In the case of Central, the high population density and changing topography have inspired years of intricate infrastructural network development. At the human scale, the footbridge system is the manifestation of a relationship that is tightly interlaced with the city fabric. This system becomes the place for a project for a city museum.

As an alternate form of public space, this city museum includes three modes of learning about culture. First, it animates learning with the bustling ambience of the wet market and financial district. They are characterized by an influx of pedestrians against the backdrop of one-hundred-year-old shophouses. Two community centers are designed for recreational learning, along with a dedicated classroom for studying local history and culture shared by local craftsmen, hawker store workers, and business owners, et al. Secondly, learning outside the footbridge can proactively engage with a historic neighborhood that includes the back streets and alleys of Central.

A deployable hawker store structure is designed for informal gatherings alongside existing hawker stores that sell second-hand collections or groceries at Tai Ping Shan Street and Lascar Row. As visitors and students ascend to the mid-levels, an observation tower is where the learning above the footbridge happens. It speaks to the contemporary living conditions in Hong Kong, yet is completely open to the public for leisure. As an alternate form of green space, the observation tower is a place for the public to enjoy the skyline. In turn, this elevated experience forms part of the kinetic learning along the footbridge and around the alleys of Central that together aim to strengthen the public's spatial sensitivity through a series of amplified collective cultural experiences.

Right: Perspective view of the observation tower

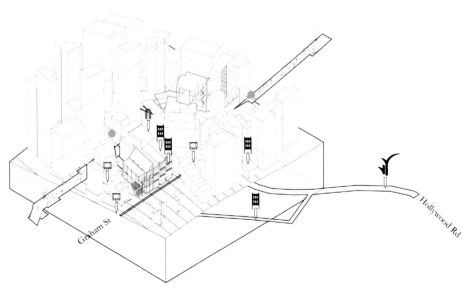

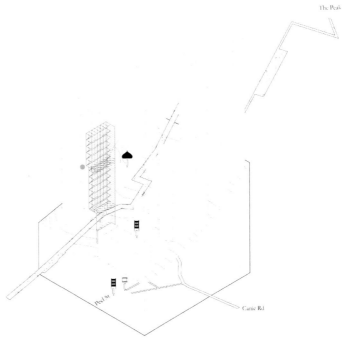

Top left: Hong Kong City Museum physical model

Top right: Learning above the footbridge diagram

Bottom left: Learning at the footbridge diagram

Bottom right: Perspective view of the Hawker stores experience

Next page left: Perspective of the community center

Next page right: Perspective of the community center along shophouses

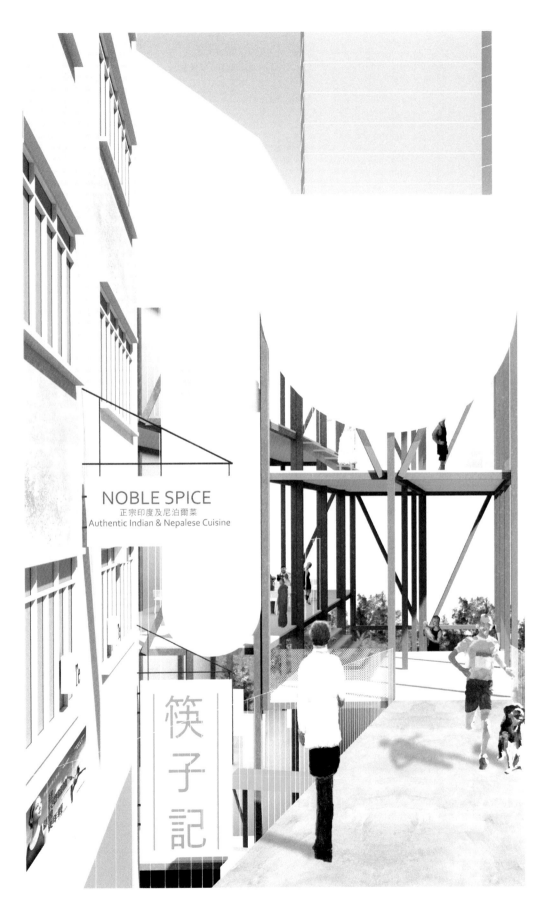

NOBLE SPICE
正宗印度及尼泊爾菜
Authentic Indian & Nepalese Cuisine

筷子記

River City

Saba Salekfard

This project imagines the rebirth of the once suppressed and forgotten Los Angeles River as a linear outdoor campus and proposes a new ecosystem as an alternative backdrop for the public life of the city's inhabitants. The Los Angeles River stretches 51 miles over the course of the city, passing through 17 cities and adjacent to around 80 schools. Many Angelenos encountering the river on a daily basis wonder what meaning and function it holds today. Such questions spurred the brief of the project, Can the L.A. River become a linear outdoor campus and a new alternate site for learning? These curiosities were first explored and questioned during the pandemic's lockdown when I began to engage with new ways of learning through explorations of the city and a self-curated curriculum. If I was able to learn through being on the site, on the street, and on the road, couldn't other Angelenos?

The proposal thus begins with an investigation into where the city's water comes from and the real threat of flooding. If the project can mitigate flooding concerns, then a curriculum can begin to evolve and develop around water in a way that incorporates multiple activities, interdisciplinaries, and diverse populations. The first portion of the curriculum covers outreach. It aims to educate Angelenos on proper water use, encouraging them to be mindful while proposing new water conservation methods. The next phase focuses on education and connecting the river to nearby schools.

The curriculum advocates for an organic development of learning through fieldwork and site visits, broken down into a series of activities spanning age groups and incorporating water-adjacent topics such as landscape, biology, and ecology. These activities are sprinkled along various routes of the river, acting as interventions that plug into existing conditions. The last phase of the project is revitalization: restoring and improving the river for public use and education. To do this, and mirroring the city's master plan, the project proposes a kit of parts, pieces that incorporate landscape and water to stimulate learning through journey and exploration. Now, larger stretches of riverbed can be covered to create riverfront parks that advocate learning through play, discovery, and an occupation of the site. River City invites nature and public activity back to the Los Angeles River and opens it up to new opportunities of learning about water and the city's history for both residents and students.

Top right: Perspective view of outdoor classroom and learning experience

Bottom right: Site isometric of Los Angeles River intervention

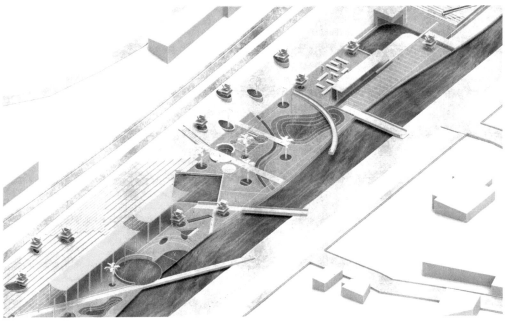

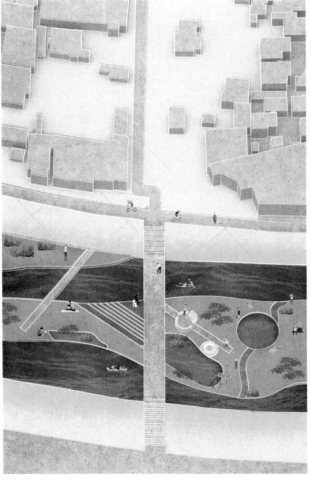

Top: Kit of parts diagram for the Los Angeles
River intervention

Left: Elysian site intervention

Right: Los Angeles River curriculum diagram

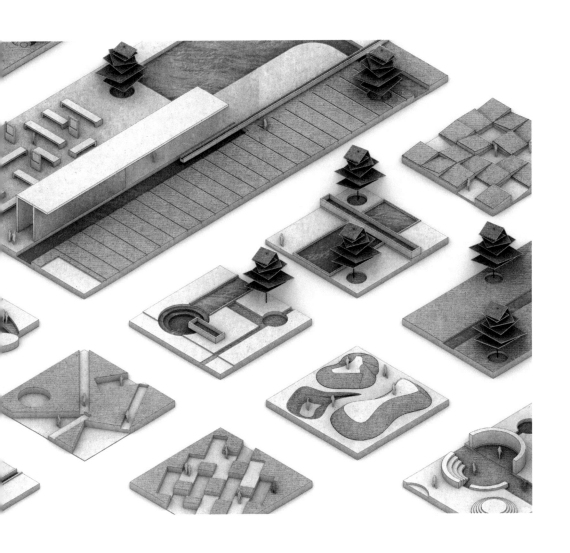

River as Classroom
A River-Based Curriculum

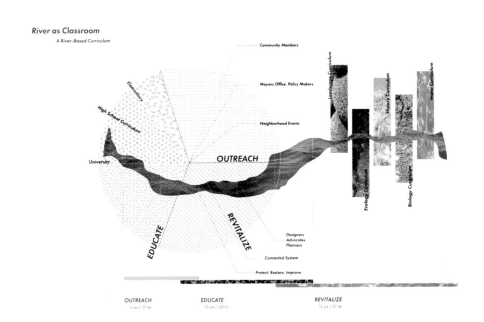

Community Members

Mayors Office, Policy Makers

Neighborhood Events

Elementary

High School Curriculum

University

OUTREACH

EDUCATE

REVITALIZE

Designers
Advocates
Planners

Connected System

Protect, Restore, Improve

Landscape Curriculum

Ecology Curriculum

History Curriculum

Biology Curriculum

Water Curriculum

OUTREACH
5 yrs / 10 mi

EDUCATE
10 yrs / 20 mi

REVITALIZE
15 yrs / 31 mi

Top: Perspective view of outdoor classroom and learning experience

Bottom: Perspective view of the Lincoln Heights site intervention

Top right: Perspective section of the Lincoln Heights site intervention

Bottom right: Site plan physical model

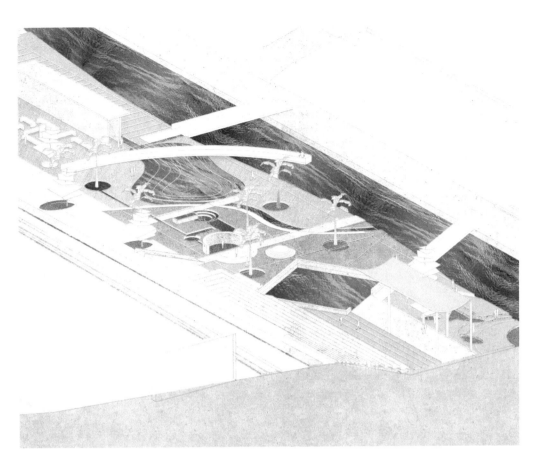

Adaptive River-Use

Tyler Krebs

By considering learning to be an essential ingredient to urban design, my proposal turns a series of abandoned industrial structures along the Cuyahoga River in Cleveland, Ohio into a dispersed network of education. The river was once the core of the city—years of industrial production along the riverbanks turned Cleveland into one of the nation's major manufacturing centers. In the 1960s, after years of abuse to the river, the city began to experience industrial decline. In 1969, symbolic of the city's economic downturn, the Cuyahoga River caught on fire. Since then, fifty percent of the population has left. The river, which once brought the city together, is now vacant, inaccessible, and strictly divides Cleveland into its East and West sides.

I mapped out the life of a typical building from its idea to its eventual demolition and found that buildings are not static objects, but rather are dynamic structures which are influenced by forces of nature, culture, governance, infrastructure, commerce, and fashion. Our learning environments should reflect this and be able to expand and contract to address present needs. They should incorporate all aspects of a circular building economy. They should continually look to engage with entities outside the profession. And they should not only seek to teach students but also be inherently intertwined with the public. This type of education would create socially responsible citizens. This type of learning environment would create community members who are globally considerate, locally engaged, and spatially intelligent.

My proposal is to make the river publicly accessible by providing easier ways to access, cross, and walk beside it. Along with this newly accessible riverfront will be a new school of the built environment. Instead of occupying a singular building, the school will be dispersed along the river and take over vacant structures with programs relating to the circular building economy. There will be spaces to learn about design, construction, and demolition, along with new lecture halls, classrooms, and a library. For example, the abandoned lower level of the Detroit-Superior Bridge will become a new pedestrian walkway with design studios and pinup spaces. Each intervention will be a resource to the public and look for ways to engage with local businesses and institutions.

The school ultimately becomes a network of site-specific learning interventions that embraces the whole of the built environment. As the school grows, or as its needs change, it can leave sites or take over new ones. New businesses and industries along the river mean new opportunities for the school to adapt and engage. Regardless of the future structure of the school, the lasting impact will be a new public core of the city where people from the East and West sides can come together and learn about the built environment.

Following page: physical model of all sites and interventions

Top: Path through gravel and construction site intervention collage

Top: Perspective view of the material processing site

Learning to be Local

Ben Thompson

In considering our modes of consumption, the supporting network of distribution centers, and big-box stores developing around infrastructures for grocery delivery service, I began to question what kind of learning can take place on the massive amount of land big-box stores take up in the American landscape. In Oakland County, Michigan, the city of Royal Oak sits on land scraped flat by the glaciers that formed the Great Lakes. The resulting fertile land was farmed by indigenous and settler inhabitants. Oakland County, a principal county of the Detroit metropolitan area, later became a prototype for suburbanization, which proliferated in the postwar period.

Frank Lloyd Wright had been commissioned to build one of the first housing blocks recognizable as a subdivision just two miles from my family home. The site of this failed project is now occupied by a Meijer superstore, just one of a pantheon of big-box stores that formed the commercial reality of my childhood. Following Wright's intervention, Cedric Price was commissioned by the nascent institution, Oakland County Community College, to conceive of a new way that this suburban educational model could be deployed across the wide swaths of land

in Oakland County. Price's idea for Oakland County Community College was to disperse the learning across the county to make it as accessible as possible. Rather than adopting the institutional model of a campus, his scheme involved occupying vacant storefronts, setting up lecture halls in parking lots, and installing a network of mobile learning pods at major intersections capable of accessing broadcast video lectures.

Big-box stores are now in their death throes due mainly to Amazon, but they still take up massive amounts of land and resources. Many other corporations also engage in predatory real estate practices known as Dark Store Theory, in which stores are intentionally built and abandoned in order to artificially lower real estate value in a given area. These practices have inspired an investigation into the idea of merging vacant big-boxes with the community college learning model, and also using their large footprint to reinstate a connection to agricultural activities practiced by previous inhabitants.

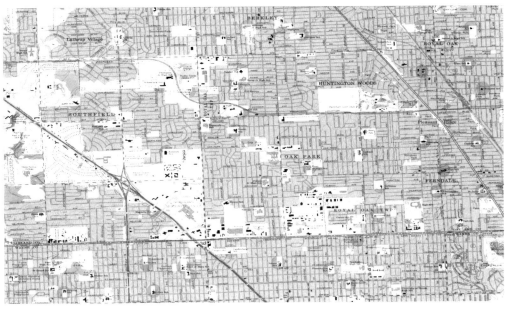

Top: The big-box store converted to an agricultural structure, the parking lots become crops

Bottom: Diagram mapping the open and closed big-box stores in Detroit, Michigan

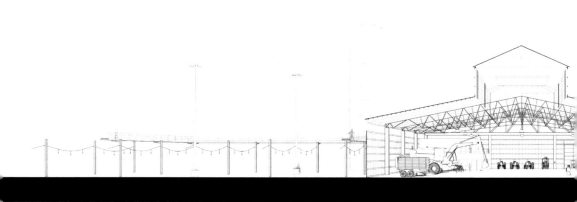

Top: A section perspective of a converted retail campus

Bottom: An interior of a big-box fitted with classrooms and workshops

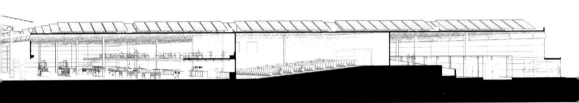

Bottom: An arboretum in the footprint of a deconstructed big-box
store

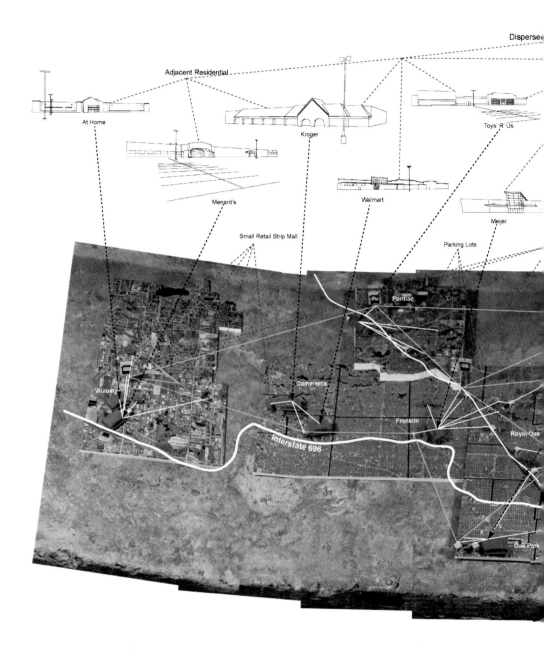

Top: Network diagram of vacant big-box retail locations in Oakland County

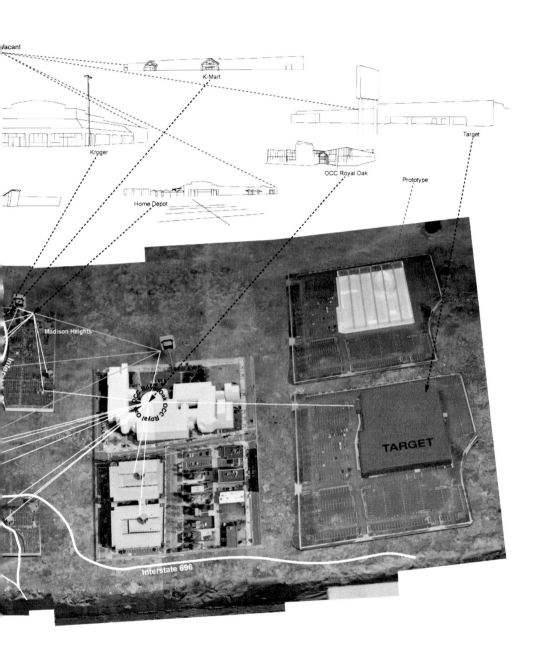

Vacant

K-Mart

Kroger

OCC Royal Oak

Prototype

Target

Home Depot

Madison Heights

OCC Royal Oak OCC Royal Oak

TARGET

Interstate 696

Interview with Deborah Saunt

Previously published in Yale's *Constructs*

Nina Rappaport (NR) How did you come to work for Colin St. John (Sandy) Wilson on the decades-long British Library project and then for MJ Long, as she was starting her own practice?

Deborah Saunt (DS) When I finished my postgraduate degree at Cambridge, there was a tradition of Sandy hiring a few graduates, so I started to work on the British Library. It was one of the few major public buildings being constructed at the time, and there I discovered this amazing person called MJ, who was instrumental in the library's design. Many of us want to correct the history books to refer to it as Sandy Wilson and MJ Long's collaboration. She was working at a time when the boys got the recognition. I was MJ's first hire when she started her practice and was traveling to Yale regularly to teach. I enjoyed that culture of a practice spanning between academia and professional projects; I just assumed that is what all architects did, and I followed in her footsteps.

NR How did you decide to start your own studio with your life partner, David Hills?

DS David and I studied at Cambridge and worked with MJ and Sandy at different times, so we shared that lineage. In between, I worked with Tony Fretton, who talked about politics, poetry, society, and public life as well as building. This experience helped me determine where I wanted the practice to go, and David shared these aims. While I was a student I produced my own projects, which made me understand that the preoccupations you have in your earliest period will probably remain abiding themes: the architecture you choose to engage with is an amplification of your understanding of your own place in the world.

NR You were lucky to have women as mentors. How did that affect the way you see yourself as an entrepreneur and practitioner?

DS I had always worked with female architects. I had a mother who worked and a grandmother who built, so I never thought of it as anything other than a calling. The gender issue didn't really surface until I got into the workplace and was disappointed to find that architecture was, and still is, very pale and male. I have manifested my interest in addressing diversity by helping to establish a prize in the name of Jane Drew, now run by the *Architecture Review*, and later co-founding the London School of Architecture, which aims to redress underrepresentation in architectural design and city making.

NR With its focus on working almost solely in London, DSDHA (Deborah Saunt David Hills Architects) has gained a deep understanding of the city. How have your projects been guided by the context of the periphery and the shape of London's streets and open spaces? In turn, how do your buildings and urban projects influence the context as a give-and-take between building and urban environment?

Top left: MJ Long at the Yale School of Architecture, 1989

Bottom left: Students from the first cohort entering the London School of Architecture, 2015

Next page: St Anne's SureStart Centre, DSDHA, 2007

DS That is a really good question. Initially, our projects were very disparate and spread across the country, and only later became increasingly urban and focused on complex settings. Early on, we were fortunate enough to win competitions for education buildings, which over five years led us from kindergartens to a Cambridge University building—all pavilions. For my PhD in practice a few years ago at RMIT (Royal Melbourne Institute of Technology), I analyzed how pavilions in remote areas and dense urban buildings are based on similar design principles, addressing relationships between site, context, and people. This has influenced the way we describe our role as spatial strategists and not just architects or urban designers, with a more nuanced understanding of physical networks based on dedicated research. We deploy the same methodology, analysis, and grounded research irrespective of physical context, whether looking at a nursery school on the outskirts of a poorer area in the north of England or a project in London's Mayfair district. We look at the site, environment, histories, sociopolitical and economic conditions, and then we make our proposition.

NR Scale plays an important part in your practice, from the smaller scale of a house, studio, or school to larger spatial strategies at the infrastructural scale of sidewalks, transit, and public spaces. How do these all come together for you now as urban designers?

DS We have a studio motto: "Community is context." We include people who are part of a larger constituency and put their needs in that context. We predicate all of our projects on the notion of exchange to make sure that everybody benefits from development. Through research we uncover hidden needs, and we use our projects as leverage to make improvements and as an opportunity to address environmental issues. Another motto is: "If you draw it, it can happen." So we draw the greening of streets, new pedestrian-friendly bridges and infrastructure, and we believe in the agency of architects as a way to push an urban design agenda.

NR In which public projects did you engage the community with that kind of agency, and what was your method of outreach to the residents?

Top: 3-35 Piccadilly facade model, DSDHA, 2020

Top: British Library proposal, DSDHA with RSHP, 2022

DS One method is to hold "100 conversations" with passersby near the site before starting a project. It is a huge investment, but it is an effective way to uncover the unwritten brief of an area and critically challenge our own preconceptions. We won a competition to relocate the school of Christ's College on a very large site and noticed that somebody had snipped through the fence along a playing field to make a short cut. We realized that there was a large social housing development nearby and the only route to amenities from there was through the school grounds. Through our agency as architects we won approval to put a road through the site and constituted the school around it to assist the flow of people. It was amazing to see this happen, and they even put a cycle route through it to integrate the whole district. Breaching the boundaries as we made this new public building enabled more public amenities.

NR That certainly illustrates the impact of a single building on its broader context. How did the Tottenham Court Road project address the local community's needs and gain traction as a larger economic project?

DS We won the competition to do a one-mile-long project that would radically transform Camden's West End, an area that was underperforming economically, socially, and environmentally. Our proposal was to string five amazing public spaces through the city and to detune many roads. We discovered, through the 100 conversations, that a major hospital on the site wasn't mentioned in the formal brief, and we identified a constituency of health-care workers and patients who had not been heard. As a result, we made roads more pedestrian friendly and created some healthy streets and back routes for doctors, nurses, patients, families, and visitors to leave the confines of the big hospital machine and get outside, which now is more important than ever. We also discovered that there were huge universities cheek by jowl with big business but very little conversation between the two. So we mapped all of the educational institutions in central London and showed it to the businesses, and there was a palpable intake of breath. We said, "Do you realize you have the equivalent of Oxford and Cambridge on your doorstep?" That was the beginning of what is now called the Knowledge Quarter, a knowledge-based economic zone where universities, the British

Library, and innovation-focused businesses all form a branded cluster.

NR After many months of living with the social world at a physical distance, what have you been thinking about in terms of the impact of COVID-19 on the city and the role of architects in the "new normal"?

DS We hope all architects can be embedded in their local communities. We do a lot of pro bono work through our studio's Spatial Intelligence Group. We have been working with the local authority on initiatives for low-traffic neighborhoods to encourage cycling and walking in young, diverse communities that are typically absent in formal consultations. We held a summer program for teenagers to design interventions using Minecraft as a drawing tool. Our team works with these teens to build timber projects, providing them with design and engineering skills that will allow them to shape their own environments.

NR The breadth of work in your studio is so wide, with new projects at the high end of the spectrum in terms of visibility and cost, such as Piccadilly for the Crown Estate, alongside local projects. How do you manage to go back and forth between clients with different economic levels and strategies?

DS We are kind of Robin Hood architects, alternating between not only different scales but also economic extremes. We work in the wealthy city center and on the periphery, where we are co-designing the modernist housing Tustin Estate, in South London, as an urban revitalization project. Other architects entered the competition with finished designs; we went in with just an open ear to listen to the residents and learn how we could design with them.

NR What was your focus in your Yale studio this fall? How did you approach teaching in the time of COVID-19?

DS We are very interested in the condition of dispersed learning in public and in public space. We looked at how learning has taken place in the past and the form it might take in the future, addressing particularly what is happening now in terms of architecture and the environment. We used spatial strategies to look at the networks between us and the new civic movement that uses the street and its publicness as a site of protest and information exchange. We started with Rudolph Hall and how it functions as a hub for networks between the personal, the urban, and the virtual. The studio ran parallel with DSDHA's ongoing project for the British Library's public realm in terms of the role of public space, access to knowledge, and architecture. We have come back to Sandy and MJ as we open up that building for locals, passersby, and other diverse constituents of public spaces.

Right: Alex Monroe Studio, DSDHA, 2012

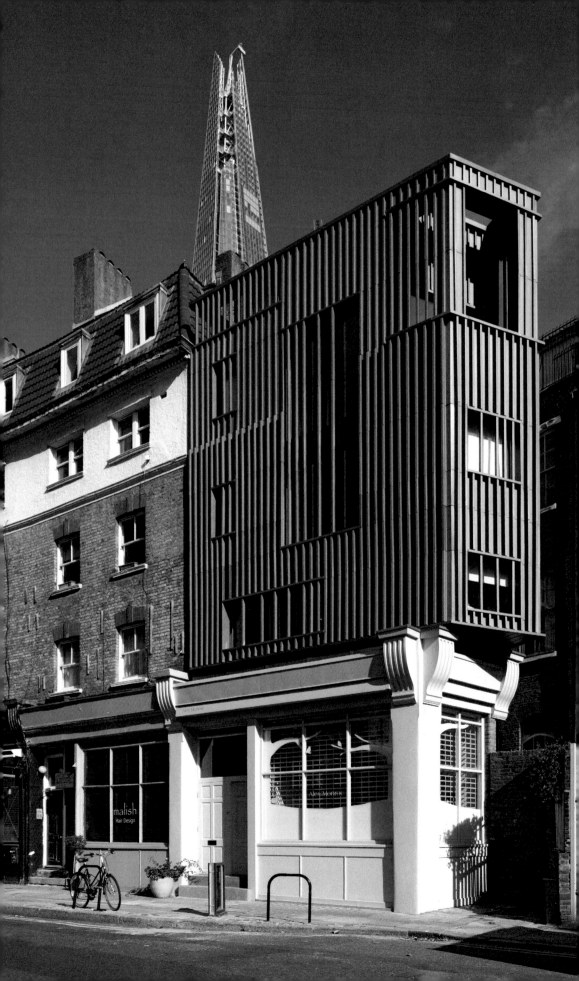

Yale School of Architecture

Conclusion

Deborah Saunt

Looking back over the past year, "What About Learning?" has transformed, first, from a question about how we learn in the midst of the intersecting crises in health, climate, and social inequality, to, second, an active affirmation that knowledge exchange about the built and natural environment should be a fundamental civic right that has to be defended and nurtured. This is true now more than ever as communities seek agency to reshape their environments in exercising their "right to the city." In our roles as architectural designers and educators, we can understand spatial justice as both an ethical imperative for fair treatment and access and an active process that we should embed in our work as we facilitate the making, sharing, and rebalancing of collective knowledge in design.

The studio took place under the extraordinary conditions of the pandemic and against the backdrop of the Black Lives Matter and Extinction Rebellion movements, as well as the 2020 U.S. presidential elections. The personal circumstances, heightened global stakes, and impacts of spatial justice informed the research and design theses of each of our tenacious and talented students as they responded to issues ranging from the sometimes gross inadequacies and loopholes in urban planning and uneven accessibility to public infrastructure and urban mobility to imminent flooding issues and their disproportionate effects on the disadvantaged. While the projects grew from each student's connection with their personal geography, they were developed with extensive site analysis and research in collaboration with interlocutors such as environmental engineer Patrick Bellew, Living City NYC, and local individuals whom they met virtually. Our three-day international symposium brought together diverse guest speakers to share their work on alternative models of spatially related learning and knowledge exchange in the realms of pedagogy, art, and activism. The event itself was an experimental learning platform. Without the prohibitive cost of travel, we were able to host a more diverse panel and audience, with some joining from bedrooms across the world in different time zones, some without any immediate affiliation with Yale University. As such, it hoped to embody the aims of the studio to open up access to greater understanding about the huge role the built environment plays in so many broader social, political, and economic issues.

Underpinned by the notion that architecture itself is an act of communication in both its process and built form, each project sought to uncover and enable new forms of exchange. They challenged the current institutional paradigm of siloed knowledge production and revealed, instead, how learning takes place not in isolation but across networks, and how architecture, at both the strategic and local levels, can facilitate different kinds of access which enable and democratize learning. The architectural proposition is not merely the designing of interventions, but of spatial strategies, such as revealing hidden resources, facilitating local spatial partnerships and alliances, and proposing new models of knowledge sharing. The result is nothing less than a new form of city making, one that moves away from expert-led, top-down planning towards new modes of co-design based on collective knowledge and spatial justice.

We believe in the notion of proto-practice—that, as students, we are already in practice and embodying the values that we will take forward beyond education. We were pleasantly surprised at the beginning of the semester to find that the majority of students in the studio had the desire to teach and share their knowledge. We wish the very best for—Ashton, Ben, Claudia, Gordon, Justin, Shuang, Saba, Tyler, and Vish—and have no doubt that they will carry further afield what they have nurtured in the studio as designers, educators, and planetary citizens.

Image Credits

Page 4, 6
Courtesy of Canadian Centre for Architecture

Page 12
Photograph by Klaus Hoppe, copyright Martin Schmitz Verlag
Photograph by Bertram Weisshaar, copyright Martin Schmitz Verlag

Page 13
Copyright The Open University

Page 14-15
Photograph by Steven Izenour, courtesy Venturi, Scott Brown, and
Associates, Inc and MIT Press

Page 17
Photography by Theo Simpson, courtesy Tom Ó Caollaí and Rory
McGrath from OK-RM

Page 20
Photograph by Vinciane Lebrun, courtesy Nelly Ben Hayoun-
Stépanian

Page 22, 23
Photography by Nick Balloon, courtesy Nelly Ben Hayoun-Stépanian

Page 25
Photograph by Nick Balloon, courtesy Nelly Ben Hayoun-Stépanian

Page 26
Copyright Monash University

Page 28
Photograph by Halkin Mason, courtesy Leroy Street Studio
Photograph by Pankaj Khadka, courtesy Leroy Street Studio

Page 30
Copyright Robert Mull

Page 33
Copyright Joel de Mowbray

Page 35
Copyright Alicia Pivaro

Page 36
Photograph by Dennis Graef, courtesy RESOLVE Collective

Page 38
Photograph by Vishnu Jayarajan, courtesy RESOLVE Collective

Page 130
Copyright Rolfe Kentish
Photograph by Emma Gibney, courtesy DSDHA

Page 132
Photography by Edmund Sumner, courtesy DSDHA

Page 134, 135
Copyright DSDHA

Page 137
Photograph by Dennis Gilbert, courtesy DSDHA

Biographies

Deborah Saunt
Eero Saarinen Visiting Professor

Deborah Saunt is a Founding Director of the architecture, landscape and research studio DSDHA. Known for their high-profile urban strategies and innovative buildings, they have been recognised with 20 RIBA Awards to date, shortlisted for the RIBA Stirling Prize, and twice nominated for the European Union Prize for Contemporary Architecture – Mies van der Rohe Award. Much of her current work is concerned with democratising architecture and helping to redefine its role in the twenty-first century—addressing people's emerging needs in the context of rapidly shifting environmental, technological, and social conditions. Deborah gained her PhD with the RMIT Practice Research Programme, a Fellowship in the Built Environment from the Royal Commission for the Exhibition of 1851, and has held academic appointments at École Polytechnique Fédérale de Lausanne, the University of Cambridge, and the London School of Architecture, of which she is a founding director.

Jane Wong
Research Assistant

Jane Wong is an architect and researcher working across design, visual culture, and writing. Her work focuses on the relationships between familiar and neglected histories, social and political processes that shape landscapes and the built environment. She is the co-author and lead researcher of *Towards Spatial Justice: A guide for achieving meaningful participation in co-design processes* (2022, RIBA and UCL-funded) and *Co-designing Public Space: In Policy and Practice* (forthcoming, funded by the British Council). She has practised in Berlin and London, where she led numerous public realm projects and strategic visions for estates and the cultural sector, such as the Royal Albert Hall and the Portman Estate, and research studies on accessibility and inclusivity. She teaches at the Bartlett School of Architecture on several programes, including the pilot MSci programme and the MA Architecture and Historic Urban Environments. She was born in Hong Kong and studied at the Architectural Association.

Timothy Newton
Senior Critic

Timothy Newton is a Senior Critic and the Director of the Yale School of Architecture's fabrication shop.